# The Essential Presence

# The Essential Presence

## 40 Days to Increased Intimacy with God

Bill Elliff

*Graceful Truth Series*
*Volume 2*

THE ESSENTIAL PRESENCE
By Bill Elliff

Graceful Truth Series | Volume 2

Published by TruthInk Publications
6600 Crystal Hill Road
North Little Rock, Arkansas 72118



Cover Design | Keith Runkle

Cover Photo | Daniel Elliff

ISBN: 0983116830
ISBN: 9780983116837

*Printed in the United States of America*



TRUTHINK
publications

**Dedicated to My Children**

*Jennifer, Rebecca, David, Joshua*
*Bethany, Daniel, Timothy, Jessica*
*And their great spouses*
*and the growing number of near-perfect grandchildren.*
*(May the tribe increase!)*

*My highest prayer for each of you is that you will*
*all know the Essential Presence.*

## BEFORE YOU BEGIN ...

There's just something about 40 days. All through history, God has led his people into 40 day adventures. Moses came apart for 40 days; Jesus fasted 40 days. Most often, these are times when God has called his servants apart to encounter the presence of God.

It would follow that God has some 40 day adventures for us. The Lord has led me on multiple occasions into 40 day seasons. Perhaps it is because God knows it takes about six weeks to build a habit. Or, that the voices around us are so strong that we need that much time to be weaned from this world and recalibrated to God's voice.

All our books in the Graceful Truth Series are designed around this 40 Day rhythm. You could read them in less time, but, along with your normal Scripture reading, these books are created to be read one chapter a day, with a good mix of prayerful, thoughtful meditation and response.

Each book focuses on a key area of spiritual life. This book challenges you to the most important step: to dramatically increase your intimacy with God. Hopefully it could be a source you return to often over the years when you sense a dry season in your spiritual walk or find yourself with a growing distance from Christ.

Nothing could be more important. I pray you will read this slowly, deliberately, and prayerfully. Ask God to help you discover afresh the beauty and power of His Essential Presence. May He thrill you with Himself, once again.

Bill Elliff
Maumelle, AR
June 13, 2017

# DAY 1

## THE ESSENTIAL PRESENCE

*And He said, "My presence will go with you, and I will give you rest." And he said to Him, "If your presence will not go with me, do not bring us up from here. For how shall it be known that I have found favor in Your sight, I and Your people?"*

*(Exodus 33:14-16)*

IT IS A blessing to know gifted men and women in life. They complete you, adding the richness of their lives and the uniqueness of their perspectives. Each friend and family member is a blessing. But there is One whose presence with you is essential above all else.

### THE PRESENCE WITH MOSES

Moses knew this well. He had known moments without God's presence and watched people live in isolation from God. He had also experienced intimacy with the Almighty.

Moses called the tabernacle the "tent of meeting" because it was designed in his day as a recognizable place of

God's presence. "Everyone who sought the Lord would go out to the tent of meeting" (Exodus 33:7b).

Moses himself would go there and God would descend, signified by the pillar of cloud standing at the entrance. It was said that Moses would commune with God "face to face, as a man speaks to his friend." The people would stand at their tent doors and worship the One who condescends to be close with those He has created.

Can you imagine what Moses experienced? The Lord had chosen to speak with him in special ways because of his unique position as the leader of God's people. Moses needed this. Only the presence of God would keep Moses centered, confident of God's direction, and intent on His glory. God's presence was his companion and compass in an amazingly difficult journey as he led several million, ever-grumbling Hebrews to the Promised Land.

And Moses knew that only God among them provided their distinctiveness. Apart from His presence they would have been just another pagan people, doomed to a separated, wandering, idolatrous life.

## THE PRESENCE WITH YOU

Moses' experience was unique, but not unrepeated. For the sacrifice on the great altar of Golgotha, which the tabernacle foreshadowed, brought salvation to all men. The veil of the temple was torn in two on that day, symbolizing the ability for all believers to enter the Holy of Holies and experience the Presence.

And then at Pentecost the Father bestowed His Spirit upon His children. "I will not leave you orphans ... I will be with you and will be in you," Christ proclaimed (John 14:17-18). He fulfilled that glorious promise, making each believer the temple of the Holy Spirit.

We can experience the essential Presence! We can know God! We can commune with Him as friend to friend! It is the great condescension His matchless mercy provides. But it is also a sign that we were created for this. His Spirit in us now and heaven in our future proves that God delights in *our* presence. He enjoys our fellowship and welcomes us to Himself.

Relish His presence. Let nothing abort this communion. Delight in each God-filled hour and the amazing opportunity to commune with the Creator of the universe.

And at the end of each day bow in humble gratitude, for you have been given the greatest privilege and the highest honor. You have experienced the Essential Presence.

## DAY 2

# THE AVAILABILITY OF GOD

*As for you, my son Solomon, know the God of your father ... If you seek Him, He will let you find Him.*

*(1 Chronicles 28:9)*

God wants to be known. Accessibility is His most remarkable attribute. That the God of the universe would condescend to human understanding is astounding.

### LETTING US IN

He backs up His desire by aggressive self-disclosure. Never waiting for us, He displays His mercy in every cloud, His grandeur from every mountain, His refreshment in fall breezes, and His surprising power in spring tornados. Day by day His creation brings forth speech.

He's gone to extraordinary lengths to give black-and-white revelation. His Word unveils His character with every stroke of the pen, just as your words reveal you. He can be known through the Bible. In fact, that's the point—over

1,000 God-breathed pages that say, "Here I am and this is what I'm like."

If that were not enough, He laid aside all His rights and privileges as God and poured Himself into human flesh. "The Word of God became flesh and dwelt among us and we beheld His glory" (John 1:14). God was saying, "Do you want to know Me? What I think, how I act, what I value, what I invest in, what matters? Then look at my Son," and there He was in human flesh.

As Jesus interacts with a group of children, we view His compassion; with Peter, His stability; with Mary Magdalene, His grace. A fuller picture has never been painted. "If you've seen Me, you've seen the Father," Christ said.

And His Spirit helps us in our weakness. How could we ever view God through filthy lenses smudged by sin? So, He blows through our minds with the purifying wind of His Spirit and the washing of the water of the Word … enlightening, convicting, communicating. "Things which eye has not seen, nor ear heard, nor which have ever even entered the heart of man … God reveals them through His Spirit."

What amazing portraits He gives so we may know Him!

## HIS ONE REQUEST

For all of this He asks one thing: "Seek Me." He asks us to lay aside other vain affections which will produce nothing of value and make the main occupation of our lives the pursuit of the Holy. We need this constant call, for our heads are easily turned by Satan's sequined substitutes.

John Piper said, "Whatever has entranced you or captivated you or swallowed up your attention, it is the haze of illusion if it desensitizes you to the combat between the Holy Spirit and Satan for your life and if it diverts your solemn attention from the mountains of eternity just ahead."

To know Him takes a knowledgeable and consistent resistance to the Enemy. To find Him takes time and attention. Not because He's hiding, but because our deceived minds are only slowly convinced of His value.

Those who know Him—really know Him—are the joyful few who give themselves wholly to the task, who pay the price for intimacy with the Almighty.

Why would we ever look elsewhere?

# DAY 3

## SAVING FEAR

*So the church throughout all Judea and Galilee*
*and Samaria enjoyed peace,*
*being built up and going on in the fear of the Lord*
*and in the comfort of the Holy Spirit, it continued*
*to increase.*

*(Acts 9:31)*

Why is it, in the experience of most followers of Christ, that we only know the presence of Christ intermittently? Sporadic seasons of closeness, joy, and the power of His presence?

Everything flows from the presence of the Lord. To have Him in the midst of every moment of the common day is to have everything we need. His absence means we have nothing of value.

We may know this, but still allow the daily routine of our lives to evidence a conspicuous lack of Him. We cry out to Him in times of crisis. But why do most of us fail to live in the atmosphere of God's presence continually?

## THE RECOGNIZABLE EXPERIENCE

Some men and women stand apart as those who have gained a higher level of experience. To be around them is to almost always encounter God. Their clothing—like the priests in the temple who conducted sacrifices in His presence—has the supernatural fragrance of the Son of God who is walking with them everywhere. These believers seem to live each day, *all day* in the rarefied air of Christ. They do not walk in perfection, but in a more intense communion with Christ.

When they listen to you, you feel as if they are peering into your soul like God Himself. When they talk, God-initiated words seem to wash over you that are amazingly "fit for the need of the moment, which give grace to those who hear." There is an economy of motion in their lives. Things get accomplished in Divine timing and power. They seem to be walled about with peace.

We can mark this off as some unique gift—that God has anointed some above others—and thus excuse ourselves from the search for this hourly intimacy with God. But one must believe, if he believes the Bible at all, that this is not to be an anomaly. Every believer is promised this possibility.

You have "everything you need for life and godliness" through God's promises and empowering presence, said Peter. Paul said we can do "all things through Christ" and that He has "blessed us with every spiritual blessing in the heavenly places in Christ." It is ours for the taking. In fact, the Father expects it of every believer. "Walk worthy of the high calling with which you have been called."

## THE IDENTIFIABLE REASON

If you are blessed to know some of these men and women, you will notice something distinct about them. They have *deliberate intention* toward God all day long. They are communing with him constantly.

> *"Many have found the secret of which I speak and … constantly practice this habit of inwardly gazing upon God. They know that something inside their hearts sees God. Even when they are compelled to withdraw their conscious attention in order to engage in earthly affairs, there is within them a secret communion always going on. Let their attention but be released for a moment from necessary business and it flies at once to God again."* (A.W. Tozer, "The Pursuit of God")

The difference is not only a deep humility that understands their spiritual poverty apart from Christ and an intense focus that turns quickly to the inner room of God's presence, but they are "going on" in this. It is sustained. There is a holy jealousy for God's presence. A circumspection about their lives. A seriousness about anything that might abort their communion with Him.

## THE FEAR OF GOD

They fear God. Understanding the holiness of the Lord, they know that much of what we casually engage in can grieve and quench the Holy Spirit. Things others tolerate, laugh at, and attend are not on their agenda.

They may even seem prudish to the unthinking Christian. But they are gaining what others only dream about. They are cautious about God's presence lest anything interrupt the sublime joy they experience with Him. This healthy fear saves them from a life of mere humanity. It delivers them from looking and acting just like the rest of the world. From a life without God in the equation.

The early church knew this. They were "*going on* in the fear of the Lord and the comfort of the Holy Spirit and they continued to increase" (Acts 9:31). God's presence was theirs and God's power was visible. Many people were being saved daily. In fact, when a little bit of hypocrisy threatened the flow of God's presence, a husband and wife were instantly disciplined by God's hand. Ananias and Sapphira would not be allowed to abort the manifest presence of God among His people. Too much was at stake. And the people who lived continually in God's presence understood this.

We may laugh at such seriousness, but when was the last time people were daily added to your church?

## DAY 4

# THE GRACE EQUATION

THERE IS PERFECT order with God. Nothing is done without intention and design. The physical world illustrates this dramatically. Each planet is perfectly placed to fulfill its destiny. Our earth, if tilted just a few degrees one way or the other would burn up or freeze. God is extraordinary in creativity and nothing contradicts His ultimate design.

## YOU'RE NOT AN ACCIDENT

Would you expect that God would leave His highest creation to chance? That man would be forgotten in this Divine plan? Scientists who understand God marvel at the physical phenomena of God's order in the human body. When two human cells, one from a mother and one from a father, form into one cell to create a life, DNA connections occur with staggering precision. Over three billion characters are created that make a one-of-a-kind-you. Miraculous accuracy from a Perfect Creator.

So what about the day-to-day living of your life? Can you imagine God creating the whole universe, with man at the apex as the ruler of this earth, without a course for man to follow? Would a perfect Creator design man and then just say, "Well, you're on your own from here"?

## THE AVENUE OF GRACE

Like all of creation, God has equations and systems for relationships, decisions, community, families, leadership—for every step of the journey. One of the greatest of these is the grace equation.

*"But He gives a greater grace.*
*God is opposed to the proud,*
*but gives grace to the humble."*

*(James 4:6)*

As opposed to a rigid program, God's plan for man's life is governed by one primary design: *connection to His Presence.* Man's inadequacies are overcome through God providing all the desire, power, and resources to His children as each need arises. Everything they need to think, decide, feel, move, and lead is found through this intimate relationship. Just as in the Garden of Eden, man can walk with God throughout the day. In this way, God is the Leader and Head, and man reigns over the sphere of his responsibilities under the Designer's perfect direction and empowering.

The bridge upon which these resources travel is called "grace." Grace is the merciful activity of God towards undeserving people that gives us the desire, power, and resources to live as He designed. Grace defines the Father's attitude (mercy) and His action (abundantly giving everything we need to live.)

Without the dynamic of grace, you cannot do what you are designed to do. This is why Paul said, "I am what I am by the grace of God," and, "His grace is sufficient."

## THE GATE

... to enter this bridge is humility. Pride ("I can do it myself," in its multiple forms) keeps the gate closed to God's gifts that are essential for living rightly. Humility ("Lord, I desperately need You!") opens the gate for God's grace to flow to our need.

God is so committed to His children operating in this dynamic relationship that He promises to oppose us if we resist. He is mercifully and relentlessly committed to us learning that we cannot live properly without Him. He spent 40 years helping an entire nation understand that, "Man does not live by bread alone, but man lives by everything that proceeds from the mouth of the Lord" (Deuteronomy 8:3). His opposition to us when we live otherwise is an act of supreme love and gracious discipline. It pushes us back to His presence.

Pride brings God's opposition—humility unleashes God's grace. Pride disconnects us from the Father—humility connects. Pride is independence—humility is dependence upon the Author and Finisher of all of life. It is an unchangeable equation for our good, set in motion by the One who designed us. God's means to connect us to the Essential Presence.

## DAY 5

# FINDING THE HONOR WE LONG FOR

*A man's pride will bring him low,*
*but he who is lowly in spirit will obtain honor.*

(*Proverbs* 29:23)

*The fear of man brings a snare*
*but whoever trusts in the Lord is safe.*

(*Proverbs* 29:25)

We have an insatiable desire to be known that is hardwired into our nature. This desire is from God and is a tool to drive us to the only Source from which real significance and affirmation can come.

## GOD'S COUNTER-INTUITIVE PROCESS

Satan tells us we must get our sense of significance and success from men. Therefore, we should fear them, always looking to others for approval. This causes us to subconsciously (and consciously) keep adjusting our lives to perform in ways that gain recognition and honor before men—a man-fearing, man-pleasing spirit.

When we live with such pride (and it is pride, for the focus is on us) we will be brought low by none other than God Himself, for He opposes the proud. But if we will die to this desire to be known by men, and humbly serve God and others, we will obtain honor by none other than God Himself. It may not be the kind of honor the world treasures, but ultimately, we will be lifted far above all this world could possibly give.

God knows how to honor those who humbly serve like His Son. In fact, He says that in the kingdom of Heaven, Jesus Himself "will gird himself to serve, and have them recline at the table, and will come up and wait on them" (Luke 12:37). Can you imagine any higher honor?

## ADJUSTING OUR BYLINE

In the tremendous book, "Embracing Obscurity," the anonymous author challenges us to think about the byline behind our names that we desire. What do we long for people to know about us?

A few sobering questions remind us how deeply this desire haunts us. It can cause us to look for affirmation in all the wrong places and keep us from the restful joy that comes from embracing humility. A few of the self-evaluating questions the author suggests are below. Take a moment and write your answers to these revealing questions.

1. *When you meet someone for the first time, what is the first or most important thing you want that person to know about who you are, what you do or what you have done?*
2. *If you lost your current vocation (not just your current position) and were forced to work in a lesser-known capacity, would you feel a sense of loss, or a change in your identity?*
3. *On a scale of 1 to 10, how important is it to you that others admire you for what you do or have done in life?*
4. *How is success defined in your genre of work or performance? In other words, what would it look like for someone to "make it" in your field? Is it your goal to "make it? If not, what is your goal (if any)?*
5. *One a scale of one to ten, what role does success (as you define it) play in whether you feel you are all-around "successful" as a person? 1 = doesn't factor in; 10 = they're practically synonymous.*
6. *Do you tie your identity to any other relationships in your life? e.g., a popular boyfriend/relationship? A gorgeous wife? A Star-athlete son or daughter?*

The man or woman who has come to the end of self-focused desire finds treasure no one else possesses. Not only do they receive restful release from the incessant push to be advanced and known by others (a crippling disease), but they gain the presence of Christ. In His presence is the highest affirmation, the greatest security, the richest honor. They are finally, fully known and embraced by the only One that really matters.

# DAY 6

## YOUR OFFICE OF TRUST

GOD HAS CREATED every man for eternal purposes. Recorded in the history of heaven are their callings and a record of their work. The first chapters of the book of 1 Chronicles seem like a random genealogy, but it is there to remind us of the importance of every man who played his part. And there was a group of men—the gatekeepers—who fulfilled one of the noblest tasks.

### MORNING BY MORNING

In Israel's history, the temple was the center of the nation's life. It was the place that represented the presence of God Himself with His people. And, it was to be meticulously cared for according to clear instructions. Look at the record of the gatekeepers of the temple:

> *For the four chief gatekeepers who were Levites, were in an office of trust, and were over the chambers and over the treasuries in the house of God. They spent the night around the house of God, because the watch was committed to them; and they were in charge of opening it morning by morning.* (1 Chronicles 9:26-27)

These men were in an "office of trust." They were given the sacred responsibilities over the wealth of the house of God. Not only did they guard the things of God, but they opened the temple "morning by morning," giving access to the very presence of God.

What an incredible task! To be such a man that you would be entrusted with the treasuries of God and enabled to give access to God's presence day-by-day!

## OUR SACRED TRUST

In a real sense, every true believer holds that responsibility now. We are given a stewardship over God's possessions. Everything you own is His. It is an office of trust. God tells us in the New Testament that we are to be stewards over these things and that one thing is required of us: faithfulness. We are to do with the Master's things precisely what He desires.

For instance, the Word of God is entrusted to us. We are to "rightly divide it," taking meticulous care to say no more and no less than it declares. It is alive and active and powerful in helping us and others. What a privilege to steward this Book!

And the Spirit of God Himself resides in us if we are His. We are now the temple, housing Him in this life. We have the task of opening the door to invite others to see His beauty and holiness in and through us, morning by morning.

## WE MUST BE AWARE

Some men don't know they have these sacred tasks. Some know they have it and ignore it or deal lightly with this trust. Some take the things God has given them and squander them in self-absorbed living. Some don't take time to open the doors morning by morning into God's presence. They experience little of Him and allow others to see little of Him through their lives.

If we are called to be Christian leaders, this responsibility is even greater. Men look to us, and rightfully so, to open the gate day by day to help them access the truth of God and the life of God. And, if we have tasted of God's manifest presence in seasons of revival, we have a high calling, for many have never experienced this. How will they know what is waiting behind the door if we do not tell them and show them?

We should see our task clearly and soberly. The majority of people on this planet do not have this responsibility. It is the sole charge of those who have come to know Christ by faith.

God can do what He desires without us, of course. But in large measure, we have been entrusted with the resources of God and access to the presence of God and we are tasked to help others "taste and see that the Lord is good." How will they enter unless we open the doors morning-by-morning?

It would be an important task to serve in the White House. But the President's President has given us a greater task. This is our office of trust. God's history will record how faithful we were to this sacred responsibility.

## DAY 7

# THE DISTINGUISHABLE DIFFERENCE

*"Is it not by Your going with us, so that we, I and Your people,*
*may be distinguished from all the other people who are upon the face of the earth?"*

(*Exodus 33:16*)

It is our primary distinction. In many ways, every believer is like everyone else on the face of the earth. We have the same physical life. Spiritually, we are all fallen creatures. We are born and we will die.

Our only difference as believers—but the astounding difference—is Him.

## Lesson Learned

Moses knew this. It began at a burning bush filled with the presence of God. Laws of nature can be suspended when God is present. Things become *super*natural. Later, before Pharaoh, Moses realized that it was not the rod in his hand, but the Presence of God in the rod that worked miracles—that made the difference.

This understanding was further engrained through 40 years of wilderness wandering, as God delivered an entire nation over and over.

Moses knew, more than most ever will, that it was the presence and power of God alone that could save him and all those for whom he was responsible. He understood that there would be no power, provision, or protection without God. This is why he sought it so greatly. This is the reason the threat of the loss of God's presence (because of the people's idol worship) was of such great concern to Moses. He offered his eternal life as a substitute in his intercession. "If you will not forgive their sins ... blot me out from the book You have written," Moses pled.

## THE EVIDENCE OF HIS PRESENCE

When Moses returned from this extraordinary encounter with God, his face literally shone. Some distanced himself from him because of the glow. Not everyone will understand the uniqueness of God's presence on the face of His children. But everyone will know that something about us has changed.

When he returned, he had the one thing he needed: the confident assurance of the Essential Presence, both for him and the people he led. Nothing more was needed—nothing less was sufficient.

## DAY 8

# THE MOST AMAZING THING ABOUT GOD

*"The Lord appeared to me from afar saying,*
*'I have loved you with everlasting love,*
*therefore, I have drawn you with lovingkindness.'"*

(*Jeremiah 31:3*)

Israel was a mess. One long story of repetitive rebellion against repetitive grace. Anyone reading through the Old Testament shakes his or her head in wonder at why God put up with this band of misfits. (Until, of course, we realize that we have the same pattern.)

But even in Israel's rebellion and returns God was glorified. Against the dark backdrop of consistent failure is seen the brilliance of one of God's most unique attributes: *everlasting love.*

## THE STARK CONTRAST

Humanistic love is *temporary*-lasting affection. We love as long as we're treated right, our needs are meet, our agenda accomplished.

It doesn't take much for us to withdraw. The clearest illustration is the current divorce rate. This epidemic, in the one relationship that should show the greatest endurance "in sickness and in health, till death do us part," magnifies humanity's inability for long love.

Notice, though, in God's dealings with Israel, the "everlastingness" of God's affections. No beginning, no end. No dip or hesitation, doubt or degree. Full yesterday and full tomorrow. It is as constant as the rising sun.

Does this mean that our sin and rebellion does not affect His love for us? His love is grieved, but never diminished for those upon whom He has set His heart. Correction is given, but only as a tough extension of love. He keeps coming because He must. His very nature dictates His response. You cannot out-sin ever-lasting. Our rebellious acts against God's love are like throwing pebbles at Mt. Everest. His passion for His children is immovable and unchangeable. "Everlasting" is a word carefully chosen and perfectly coined.

And such love is aggressive. Look at 1 Corinthians, Chapter 13 for a description that is anything but passive. Divine love is kind, patient, never rude, never seeks its own way, never keeps a record of others wrongs and never fails.

If you doubt it biblically, see it practically in God's activity towards us. He "draws us with lovingkindness." Creation and all its provisions; feeding the sparrows and His sons and daughters; providing, protecting, pursuing. And the greatest definition of ever-lasting love? "While we were yet sinners,

Christ died for us … while were His enemies we were reconciled to God by the death of His Son."

How could this possibly be? It's God. It's everlasting. It's Divine love.

## IMPLANTED LOVE

If that were not enough, in the highest stroke of grace God's love has planned a way for us to return the affection. "I will put My law within them and on their heart I will write it; and I will be their God and they will be my people" (Jeremiah 31:33).

God has ordained that His children receive a transplant, placing a new heart of Divine love within them that replaces their heart of stone. We can love now with an adoration that does not end. We do not know what we shall be like, but we shall be like Him one day soon. He will not stop until this transformation is completed in us.

Gradually now, and one day in fullness, He will receive a return on His investment. But our weakness in love now does not deter Him, and the prospect of future love does not drive Him.

He loves us because His love is everlasting.

**DAY 9**

# LEADING FROM INTIMACY

OF ALL THE attributes of Christ as a man on this earth, there was one of highest importance. The success of His mission depended entirely upon a singular practice. Everything Christ did relied on His intimacy with the Father.

The sensitive Apostle John, who most closely observed Christ, tells us its importance through repetition (John 5:30; 8:28-29, 42-43; 12:48-50; 14:9-10). Look at one example:

> *Jesus said to him, "Have I been so long with you, and yet you have not come to know Me, Philip? He who has seen Me has seen the Father; how can you say, 'Show us the Father'? Do you not believe that I am in the Father, and the Father is in Me? The words that I say to you I do not speak on My own initiative, but the Father abiding in Me does His works. (John 14:9-10)*

## THE PURPOSE OF PRAYER

Why, for instance, did Christ feel the need to pray unceasingly? He knew the path for His earthly life was to listen to the Father and do what He said. To do everything by God-initiation. This necessitated continual communion.

This illustration should clarify the Christian life for us. It is not our best thoughts *for* God, but the great thoughts *from* God that matter the most. Not activity we generate, (thereby receiving the glory), but God-initiated work. The only way to have this life is to live in the atmosphere of intimacy with God. To experience the Essential Presence. In that light, how could we spend less time praying than Christ?

As Christians, we should not ask anyone to follow our lead or take our counsel unless we are living under this intimately-gained, Divine initiation. How could we be so arrogant as to expect otherwise? A.W. Tozer advised people to "Listen to no man who fails to listen to God."

> *"This rule of listening only to those who have first listened to God will save us from many a snare. All religious projects should be tested by it. Before we follow any man we should look for the oil on his forehead. We are under no spiritual obligation to aid any man in any activity that has not upon it the marks of the cross. No appeal to our sympathies, no sad stories, no shocking pictures should move us to put our money and our time into schemes promoted by persons who are too busy to listen to God."* (A. W. Tozer, "Root of the Righteous")

Christ could summarize His human life with one statement: "If you have seen me, you've seen the Father." This is the type of men we must follow. This is the type of man we must be.

## OUR BEST GIFT TO GIVE

Can we say this? The world doesn't need more of us—they need the wisdom, love, and counsel that comes from God. It is our great privilege to "hold this treasure in earthen vessels." But we can be conduits through which the God of the universe is seen and glorified if we are men and women who think and dream, live and move, speak and act from intimacy with Him.

## DAY 10

# SEEING JESUS

*Now there were some Greeks among those who were going up to worship at the feast; these then came to Philip, who was from Bethsaida of Galilee, and began to ask him, saying, "Sir, we wish to see Jesus." Philip came and told Andrew; Andrew and Philip came and told Jesus.*

*And Jesus answered them, saying, "The hour has come for the Son of Man to be glorified. Truly, truly, I say to you, unless a grain of wheat falls into the earth and dies, it remains alone; but if it dies, it bears much fruit.*

*He who loves his life loses it, and he who hates his life in this world will keep it to life eternal. If anyone serves Me, he must follow Me; and where I am, there My servant will be also; if anyone serves Me, the Father will honor him.*

*Now My soul has become troubled; and what shall I say, 'Father, save Me from this hour?' But for this purpose I came to this hour. 'Father, glorify Your name.'"*

*(John 12:20-28)*

DO YOU LONG to see Jesus? In your life? Your ministry? Your family? Your church? Your community? To see Him is to see salvation, deliverance, truth, grace ... life itself. And you will see things in His presence that can be found nowhere else.

If you long to see Him, then you must go where He is. You will never observe Him while reclining in the easy chair of self-indulgence. Nor will you encounter him in the fast-paced boardroom of self-interest or strutting around the bright lights of self-glory.

## DIVINE MOVEMENT

You must stay up with Jesus. If you are to see His works, you must go on His path. You must follow Him. Stooping down to lift an adulterous woman, feeding 5,000 who are hungry, walking to a tomb so a friend may be raised, rising early to meet with His Father a great while before day, heading to a dinner with someone no one else will tolerate, spending all night in prayer, walking up the hill of Golgotha.

"The night is coming when no man can work; work while there is still day ... I have meat to eat that you know not of; my meat is to do the will of my Father ... I came not to be served, but to serve ... Take up your cross and follow Me," are the words you will hear if you are privileged to stay close to Him.

## DIVINE FRUIT

Follow Jesus and you will see Him bear fruit. Where He is, lives are changed. Supernatural winds blow where Jesus walks, for His Father has given Him the Spirit without measure. And everywhere Jesus is, the Father is glorified.

Do you want to see Jesus? Then you must make a determined turn from a life of self-direction and run to the Savior. It will be a challenge to stay up with Him for He is relentless in His pace. But nowhere else will you see His equal or be changed into His likeness.

# DAY 11

## THE PURPOSE OF GOD'S DELIVERANCE

*"You yourselves have seen what I did to the Egyptians, and how I bore you on eagles' wings and brought you to myself. Now therefore, if you will indeed obey my voice and keep my covenant, you shall be my treasured possession among all peoples, for all the earth is mine; and you shall be to me a kingdom of priests and a holy nation. These are the words that you shall speak to the people of Israel."*

*(Exodus 19:4-6 ESV)*

THE CURSE OF our lives is our separation. Sin takes us away from the Presence. It pulls us in directions of our choosing toward the great Rebel Enemy of God, Satan himself.

God, in His incredible mercy, reaches down and redeems us. He isn't obligated to do this, nor owe this saving work to us. And we certainly do not deserve it. What compels Him is His name. He is the Redeemer. It is one of the most precious of His many names and, in itself, is an inadequate human word to describe the magnitude of this deliverance.

## CARRIED

"I bore you on eagles' wings and brought you to Myself" is a statement of Divine activity and purpose. He lifted the Israelites from an impossible captivity, even plundering the Egyptians of their goods. The captives paid the slaves to go.

But where was God taking them? What was the point of their deliverance? "And brought you to Myself." It was (and always is) to Him. He wants us. He desires us to leave the leeks and onions of Egypt and find the milk and honey of His presence. The fullness of His life. The sufficiency of His enough-ness. The satisfaction of simple, pure devotion to Him.

## VALUED

Along the way, if we follow Him and keep His covenant, we will find we are His "treasured possession among all peoples" for all the earth is His. He has no lack in His treasury, and the meek that submit to His rule will truly inherit the earth.

The eagle may be waiting to lift you up and redeem you at the Lord's instructions, for He owns the eagles. Just remember where you are headed. Your Redeemer is winging you to Himself.

## DAY 12

# BE READY AND COME UP IN THE MORNING

OUR GREATEST MISCONCEPTION is that God is uninterested in us. From the beginning, our Ancient Enemy has deceived us into thinking that God is holding out on us and that He has no interest in our fellowship.

But the testimony of Scripture, and of men and women who have known Him, shatters this lie like a hammer shattering a rock.

> *"So be ready by morning, and come up in the morning to Mount Sinai, and present yourself there to Me on the top of the mountain." (Exodus 34:3)*

## THE DIVINE INVITATION

Moses was invited by God, as a representative of the people, into the presence of God. He was to take no one with him. It was a solitary step, but it was to be the first business of the day to enter the presence of the Almighty.

God gave Him time to prepare for this meeting. "Be ready," God said, knowing that Moses must make deliberate plans if he was not to miss this Divine encounter.

When Moses cooperated, "The Lord descended in the cloud and stood there with him as he called upon the name of the Lord" (Exodus 34:5). There on that sacred spot, God revealed Himself as the "Lord, the Lord God, compassionate and gracious, slow to anger, and abounding in lovingkindness and truth; who keeps lovingkindness for thousands, who forgives iniquity, transgression and sin" (Verses 6-7). Every word of that description is inviting. "Meet me in the morning," God said, "And I will show you who I am."

## THE NATURAL RESPONSE

Moses did what hundreds before had done and millions in succeeding years would imitate. He "made hast to bow low toward the earth and worship" (Verse 8). When we stand in God's holiness, we realize there is no one like Him. We understand our difference and we realize that He alone deserves our unashamed adoration.

And Moses' prayer when he met with the Almighty was for God's continued presence. That God would accompany His people. That He would go along in their midst and not forsake them, for a moment in God's manifest presence makes you want ten thousand more.

## THE PRESENT CALL

Men and women throughout the ages have heard God's invitation. Many have failed to respond. They have not made themselves ready. They have not come up in the morning to Mount Sinai and the results are tragic. They live lives of quiet desperation, never having the one thing that would equip them to do everything.

They have missed the Essential Presence.

## DAY 13

# THE SELECTIVE BLINDNESS OF A MERELY LATERAL VIEW

*But as for me, my feet came close to stumbling, my steps had almost slipped. For I was envious of the arrogant as I saw the prosperity of the wicked. If I had said, "I will speak thus," behold, I would have betrayed the generation of Your children. When I pondered to understand this, it was troublesome in my sight until I came into the sanctuary of God; then I perceived their end.*

*(Psalm 73:2-3, 15-17)*

NOTHING MAKES SENSE when seen from a merely human perspective. This is why educators and scientists, and even so-called theologians who take God out of the equation, can never hope to find the whole answer. We were designed to live and reason in concert with our Creator.

> *"God made us: invented us as a man invents an engine. A car is made to run on petrol [gasoline], and it would not run properly on anything else. Now God designed the*

> *human machine to run on Him. He Himself is the fuel our spirits were designed to burn. There is no other.* (C.S. Lewis, "The Weight of Glory")

If we try to make sense of anything apart from the Vertical, like the Psalmist trying to understand why the wicked seem to prosper and the righteous do not, we are in trouble. It is like an ant trying to comprehend the landscape of a metropolitan city.

## HIS OPENING

But the joyous reality is that God longs for us to know Him and His mind on all matters that we need to understand. He has given us His Word and His Spirit to open, for the humblest of His children, what is true. Like a beam of sunlight through dark clouds, He gives us pockets of profound perspective into His glory.

We look at the microscopic intricacies of a human cell or the massiveness of constellations and are baffled to understand how this could all be created … until we look to God for insight. Suddenly it all makes sense: how it could happen and why it did happen.

## OUR POSTURE

If you are walking through this world trying to grasp life apart from Him, you will be perplexed. In your confusion, you will make wrong assumptions about life that can lead to terribly destructive responses. You will either give up on understanding, or create substitute explanations that can be silly at best. You might even get angry with God and hold the only One who can help you at arms' length.

The tragedy is, you don't have to live in such darkness. God has "gladly chosen to give you the kingdom" (Luke 12:32). He has things which eye has not seen and ear has not heard prepared for those who love Him. He is waiting to renew your mind and make you wise beyond comprehension, if you will simply join Him in His sanctuary. In the Essential Presence, you will see clearly.

# DAY 14

## YOUR CALLING

*God is faithful, through whom you were called into fellowship with His Son, Jesus Christ our Lord.*

*(1 Corinthians 1:9)*

WHEN WE ENTER a new job we often receive a job description. Either verbally or written, we are told what the job is all about and what our role is to be. Who we relate to is also explained—those who supervise us and those who we lead. Without this, we would be wandering and ineffective.

### OUR PRIMARY TASK

Paul, in the beginning of the letter to the Corinthians, reminds the true Christian of the purpose of Christ's redemptive work: *We are called into fellowship with Jesus Christ, our Lord.*

The word "fellowship" is "koinonia" in the Greek language and literally means the "sharing of common life." It describes our connection—that we are united in a unique, organic way. We are in Christ and Christ is in us. We share His life, immediately and eternally.

## THE GLORY OF FELLOWSHIP

The ramifications of this union are breathtaking. Everything that Christ is and has, we have. We are "heirs and joint heirs with Him." We can talk with Him and hear Him. We are one as He and the Father are one. In fact, Jesus' lengthy prayer in John, Chapter 17, is one long plea to the Father for us, that we would understand and experience this union.

## NOT MERELY A SYSTEM

Christianity is not a system to follow, but a relationship to enjoy. It's the privilege of sharing life with Jesus. It is to be intimate, real, and constant.

The tragedy is, we don't realize what we have, now that we have Him. We revert back to our previous lifestyle of humanistic independence. It's like being married, but forgetting that union and living as if you're not joined together for life. You lose all the privileges of sharing life with your mate and the joy and fruit of that union.

Are you fellowshipping with Christ today? If not, you are living below your birthright, which was purchased at great price on your behalf. The great witness of your life to Christ is lost, and you are giving a mere caricature of true

Christianity to a world that desperately needs to see the joy of walking with Him.

## TAKE TIME

You must be deliberate to enjoy this fellowship. Like any relationship, you must give time and attention to the One who is waiting to disclose Himself to you. Some believers go for years and do not know Christ any better than they did decades before. The result? They search every counterfeit to try and find the love their heart was made to enjoy.

But if you pursue Him wholeheartedly, you will find the One who has covenanted Himself to you. You will realize He has been faithfully there in the study of your heart for years. And, if you see it rightly, you will mourn for lost hours and years of fellowship.

But after this repentance, you will find the foyer of heaven. For to share life with Him is to find heaven itself.

## DAY 15

# THE GLORY OF HIS PRESENCE

*It happened that when the priests came from the holy place, the cloud filled the house of the Lord, so that the priests could not stand to minister because of the cloud, for the glory of the Lord filled the house of the Lord.*

*(1 Kings 8:10-11)*

WE LONG FOR many things in this life. Everybody wants a little comfort, some recognition, relationships that are meaningful, someone to love and to love them, enough possessions to get by, a meaningful job.

But there is one thing that should consume our affections and desire more than all else. We should long for the presence of God.

## AN UNUSUAL MANIFESTATION

At the dedication of the first temple that was built in Jerusalem, God manifested (made clear, visible to all, undeniably seen) His presence. It was so clear that it gave the appearance of a cloud, and so strong that the men who spent their life in the service of the Lord could not stand before it.

And then there is this incredible statement: *"The glory of the Lord filled the house of the Lord."*

I have had the privilege—perhaps you have too—of being in moments where God's presence was so thick I felt I could touch it. Every time God graciously chooses to visit us in this way the results are stunning. There is a worship that is authentic and humble, for who can boast or ignore Him when He is in the house? There is genuine repentance that leads to a lasting surrender to the King. There is a spontaneous desire to tell everyone you know. Witnessing is no longer a chore, but an overwhelming compulsion.

You cannot stand in His manifest presence and be unchanged.

## A DAILY EXPERIENCE

While this cloud was an unusual appearance for an unusual moment, we should all seek His presence earnestly and daily. If we are followers of Christ, then we have the promise of His continual presence. "I will be with you and I will be in You," He promised, as He spoke of the Spirit's indwelling of every true believer.

But it is possible for the Spirit to indwell us, but be so preoccupied with the world, or grieving or quenching His

Spirit in such ways, that we lose the sense of Him and the flow of His life in and through us. We can go days unaware and unappreciative of Him. We can resist His control, foolishly thinking that our ideas and direction are superior. But nothing could be more ridiculous. Think of the days wasted when we are not pursuing His presence!

God has promised that if we would draw near to Him He would draw near to us. And His presence is what we need more than anything else on earth. The revival we long for—both for us and for the world around us—is nothing more than the return of His presence. When we experience Him, we have everything that matters and lasts. Without Him, we have nothing of value.

So why go another day, another step, another foolish decision deeper into a life without the fullness of Christ? Whatever we do today, we should do that which makes room for God.

# DAY 16

## INTIMACY WITH GOD

*"And there has not arisen a prophet since in Israel like Moses, whom the Lord knew face to face."*

*(DEUTERONOMY 34:10)*

GOD KNOWS EVERYTHING. He knows the inner workings of every cell of your body and the names of every star in the heavens. But does the Lord know you?

We speak of knowing God, but in Matthew, Chapter 7, Jesus declared that there are some who are going to stand in the judgment proclaiming their righteousness and He will say, "Depart from me—I never knew you."

### DOES THE LORD KNOW YOU?

This term indicates disclosure. It is the willingness on God's part to entrust Himself fully to you, which He gladly chooses to do for those who believe in Him. That Divine disclosure becomes more and more intimate the more we surrender to His Lordship and submit to His leadership. The more we draw near to Him, the more He draws near to us, but there are conditions on this nearness (see James 4:6-10).

We need intimacy with the Essential Presence more than we could ever possibly imagine. It is particularly true for those of us who are leaders. How can we lead others to someone we do not know? How can we describe to them the delicacies of a dish we've never tasted? How can we paint a picture of One we've never observed?

Worse yet, our souls will not be spared from the ravages of sin if we are not intoxicated with the sweetness of such intimacy. John Eldredge in "Wild at Heart" reminds us of this.

> *"Ecstasy and delight are essential to the believer's soul ... we are not meant to live without spiritual exhilaration ... the believer is in spiritual danger if he allows himself to go for any length of time without tasting of the love of Christ. When Christ ceases to fill the heart with satisfaction, our souls will go in silent search of other lovers"*

Moses was a specially selected man in God's unique economy for the deliverance of Israel. We may not expect to experience all that Moses did in this life, for Moses knew God "face to face." But there is plenty of God for you. More than you could imagine.

## HAVE YOU PAID THE PRICE OF INTIMACY?

Do you want to know God and Him to know you intimately? Would you like to be included in the inner circle of deeper intimacy with Him? And, do you believe that is possible?

We say of our deepest friends, "I know them well." We know them because we have welcomed them in as our friend and we have both paid the price of friendship.

Does God say the same of you?

## DAY 17

# GOD INITIATION

One of the greatest gifts one of my mentors ever gave me was a simple statement across a dinner table. It has affected me for decades. Almost casually, but knowing full well its potential impact, Manley Beasley leaned forward and said, "The mark of a godly man is that everything he does is God-initiated."

The Israelites, in their best seasons, were a marvelous illustration of this truth and its result.

> *And sometimes the cloud remained from evening until morning. And when the cloud lifted in the morning, they set out, or if it continued for a day and a night, when the cloud lifted they set out. Whether it was two days, or a month, or a longer time, that the cloud continued over the tabernacle, abiding there, the people of Israel remained in camp and did not set out, but when it lifted they set out. At the command of the Lord they camped, and at the command of the Lord they set out. They kept the charge of the Lord, at the command of the Lord by Moses. (Numbers 9:21-23 ESV)*

When we live with this kind of dependency, we are assured of God's presence, protection, and direction. We always arrive at the right place at the right time in the right way. This is seen in the two "all's" of a well-known passage.

> *"Trust in the Lord with ALL your heart and do not lean on your own understanding. In ALL your ways acknowledge Him and He will direct your paths." (Proverbs 3:5-6, emphasis mine)*

God is interested in us having no idol in any arena of our lives, ("all your heart"). Also, He wants us to bring Him into the equation in every single moment of the common day, ("all your ways"). He longs for this intimacy because He knows it is our only hope of success, and that, only in this dependency can we ever truly glorify God.

But there is another amazing reason for God's insistence on this tightness and it will take your breath away. He loves us! He wants to be with us. He longs for His children to walk and talk with him. We selfishly think of what we might miss if this is not practiced, but what about the Father?

## THE EXAMPLE OF THE SON

Jesus, of course, illustrated this God-initiation. In multiple accounts in the book of John, Jesus says that everything He does is by God initiation. "I do nothing on my own initiative but speak just as the Father taught me" (John 8:28).

This close order may seem like weakness to some, but it is the singular gateway to strength. The God-initiated man has all the resources of God attending him. People will recognize the difference. The glad follower will be led in "all the paths of righteousness for (God's) namesake." Sometimes it is through the wilderness, as the Israelites illustrated, and sometimes into the land of milk and honey. But always it is with Him.

To live in this way demands a life that listens. We must pay attention to God. We must be in a posture to see the cloud and pillar and the humble wisdom to follow completely. We must pursue the Essential Presence.

## DAY 18

# DEPENDENCY UPON THE DESERTED PLACE

*But the news about Him was spreading even farther, and large crowds were gathering to hear Him and to be healed of their sicknesses. But Jesus Himself would often slip away to the wilderness and pray.*

*(LUKE 5:15-16)*

EVERYTHING ABOUT THE lifestyle of Jesus should be studied and sacred to us. He not only came to show us the Father, but also to show us what a man, rightly related to the Father, must be and do.

## THE UNUSUAL PRACTICE

Jesus was drawing crowds, which is explainable. But what is not explainable is His practice to "often slip away to the wilderness (literally, the 'deserted place') and pray." Most leaders of such fame would milk the crowd moments. Or, they would tell us of their busyness and boast that they had very little time to get away, almost as a badge of their greatness. In reality, they are displaying their fatal flaw.

Jesus regularly slipped through the watching crowd and retired. This was so common for him that we can rightly say it was the deliberate habit of his life. He did this with no thought of man's opinion of His practice, but every thought of man's salvation.

## WHY SLIP AWAY?

Why would Christ not squeeze the opportunities for fame? Even his own brothers questioned him about this. But Jesus was not enamored by the crowds. He went to them because He loved people and He wanted to seek and save that which was lost.

But, His primary desire was to be with His Father and accomplish His will. Jesus knew that He could not *do* God's will if He did not *know* God's will. He knew He would have no Divine power without Divine connection and no Divine direction without Divine communion.

These hours in God's presence were the most cherished of His earthly life. He went to the wilderness because he loved His Father and longed for communion with the One He had been with forever in heaven. Quietness in the Father's presence was the goal. To simply be with the One He loved.

Every reason Jesus had for seclusion should be our reasons. The man who is always available and seeking the limelight is not the one we should follow. Follow the man, (and *be* the man), who often slips away to meet with God. This man will have something from God to tell the crowds when they appear.

## DAY 19

# GETTING READY FOR GOD

*And Joshua said, "Consecrate yourselves*
*for tomorrow the Lord will do wonders among you."*

*(Joshua 3:5)*

EVERY DAY GOD manifests Himself and most days we miss this Divine expression. We are clouded by secular cataracts and exhausted by the barrenness of a busy life.

We blow through whirlwind schedules and wonder why God never seems to speak to us; why we never see His miraculous work in our family; why we never hear His call to the extraordinary.

Even the heavens declare God's wonder with daily regularity, but for us it's just a "nice night." Our congested souls have no space for wonder.

## WE ARE RARELY READY FOR GOD

The first time the Israelites faced the Promised Land their eyes were transfixed on the size of their enemy. Blinded by fear, they could not see the Larger-than-Giants-God who would make their enemies like "bread" to them.

A whole generation missed the wonder. Wandering in the wilderness they grumbled all the way at Him for not helping them in their distress. They died without seeing the promises of God fulfilled.

The second time around Joshua made sure the next generation was prepared for God. "Consecrate yourselves," he cried, making sure they would clear room for the Almighty. "Cleanse your hearts and minds to see and follow the God who will walk among us and do wonders."

One Sunday recently two women, at separate times, approached me after the service with tears in their eyes. "This morning, in my time with God, He said ... (*this and this*). When I came this morning my heart was so full and then you spoke on the exact same truth! God is speaking so strongly to me today!"

Another had been awake early that morning burdened for her daughter. She had been prompted to write her a long note to challenge her to follow God in a difficult time. "When you began to speak," she said, "I began to weep. My daughter was right beside me and she had read my letter before church and your message was point-by-point exactly what I had been prompted to write."

They were ready for God.

It took time. They had made room in their day for Him early in the morning while others had stayed up late the night before watching a movie or playing games, struggling to get up, coming late and tired to the service, plopping down in a chair and waking up in time for the closing prayer. For those it was just a "nice service."

## THE HABIT OF SERIOUS FOLLOWERS

When you see a great Christian who always seems to be experiencing God in ways you are not, be assured they have paid a price to see God's glory. Not just for one day, but through years of accumulated consecration, their hearts have been tuned and their eyes opened to encounter Him. They have not done this perfectly, but continually over time.

What would happen if an entire congregation "consecrated themselves" every Sunday morning and gathered ready to experience God? What if they did that *every* morning? What impossible walls would collapse if Christians in a city walked into every ordinary day expecting God to do the extraordinary around them?

The prepared Israelites watched God knock down an impregnable wall and bring unheard of victory, and this was just the beginning. For centuries we have learned the truth about God through them because they were ready and obeying on the day He desired to display His strength.

What testimonies are never heard through our lives? What stories of God's greatness left untold? What walls are not coming down? What never-to-be-repeated opportunities lost? What wonders are missed simply because we are not ready for God?

# DAY 20

## THE 1:8 OPERATING SYSTEM

EVERYTHING GOD HAS taken time to record for us in the Scripture is there on purpose. We must constantly ask God, "What are you saying to me through this passage?" if we are to discover His intent for our lives. The first nine chapters of Joshua (larger than many New Testament books) give a crystal-clear picture of a vital reality.

### GOD'S OPERATING SYSTEM

The opening challenge of God to His leader, Joshua, is to listen to the Lord and follow with simple, unwavering obedience. All Joshua needed to know as they began a new life in a promised land was encapsulated in one verse: Joshua 1:8.

> *This book of the law shall not depart from your mouth, but you shall meditate on it day and night, so that you may be careful to do according to all that is written in it; for then you will make your way prosperous, and then you will have success.*

How could this be clearer and what promise could be greater? The **1:8 System.**

***(A NEW TESTAMENT PARENTHESIS:** It is fascinating to note that the New Testament also records another beginning of a new kingdom and a new system. Instructions are given in another 1:8 verse with a similar promise of God's presence. The disciples are told to wait and pray for God, listen to Him, and then move forward at His direction with an expanded promise and mission in Acts 1:8: "...but you will receive power when the Holy Spirit has come upon you; and you shall be My witnesses both in Jerusalem, and in all Judea and Samaria, and even to the remotest part of the earth.")*

## THE JERICHO LESSON

Fresh on the heels of God's 1:8 instruction, Joshua and the people face their first, and one of their biggest tests: a city with a fortress so strong that four chariots could run abreast on top of the wall. An absolutely impregnable opponent.

But Joshua discovers this is not challenge for God as he listens to the Lord and does expressly what the Great King commands. It is like a flea, effortlessly bringing down an elephant as God gives His servant a simple, bizarre plan of attack. But it works. Perfectly. Just like God said.

## THE AI LESSON

Filled with the glory of that success, they proceed to a little, nothing town of Ai. Without thinking, they send a small contingent of soldiers to take this town, but with one glaring difference: they did not inquire of God nor get His plans. They forgot the 1:8 principle.

If they would have taken this simple, critical step they would have discovered that one of their number had sinned against God. God was establishing a new kingdom in His Promised Land and needed purity of heart and intent for it to function properly. Jericho was the first fruits of the land, and the first fruits *always* belong to God. Achan's materialism and deception, exactly like Ananias and Sapphira's sin in the fledgling church in Acts, Chapter 5, threatened this whole God-society.

God withdraws His presence and protection and the entire nation is defeated until the sin is investigated and removed. Once they return to God's 1:8 operating plan, they proceed to victory.

## THE GIBEON LESSON

We return to the storyline, convinced that the Ai Lesson had its effect and the Israelites will now move only by careful listening and full dependence.

Enter the Gibeonites, who were next in the path of the conquering Israelites. These enemies of God's agenda had been made crafty by the Father of Deception who they worshiped. They pretended they were from a far country and had come to seek the Israelites protection through a covenant, which they knew Israel would be bound to keep.

And then the telling verse, placed there for our instruction, tells us the secret of Joshua's failure. It is a small verse with a massive impact and instruction.

> *So the men of Israel took some of their provisions, and did not ask for the counsel of the LORD. (Joshua 9:14)*

Satan and his followers have schemes and will trick us into alliances we should not make. His compromises always create footholds for his continued entrance into our lives and spiritual communities. And, when we do not ask for the counsel of the Lord we are mere humans trying to compete with a far superior opponent. We will lose, and the results will sometimes linger with us for decades, as the Gibeonites did with Israel.

## WILL WE LEARN?

We can read these nine chapters and be mildly challenged by the stories. Or, we can realize with sobriety that our loving God is showing us His operating system in bold relief. He gives His **1:8 System** at the beginning of both Old and New Testaments.

If we grasp this with understanding, we must not merely nod our heads and go about business as usual. We must inspect our lives and see if we are listening carefully to every Word that God is saying, meditating on it day and night, and being careful to do all that God has commanded in the power of the Holy Spirit.

Are we listening to Him before every decision, large and small? Are we pursuing the Essential Presence? Are we living under God's **1:8 System?**

# DAY 21

## ENLARGING YOUR HEART

*I will run in the way of your commandments*
*when you enlarge my heart!*

*(Psalm 119:32)*

The Triple Crown in American horse racing is considered the greatest accomplishment in thoroughbred racing. It's comprised of winning the Kentucky Derby, Preakness Stakes, and Belmont in one season by a three-year-old thoroughbred.

Only twelve horses in American history have won the Triple Crown, but none accomplished the feat quite like Secretariat in 1973. This one-of-a-kind horse crossed the finish line at Belmont in front of the entire field by 31 lengths. It is considered by many the greatest horse race in American history.

The owner of Secretariat was affected by dementia. I do not know if this is true, but in a movie centered around Secretariat's life, the owner was reported to have said to his daughter about Secretariat, "Let him run his race!"

It was an amazingly beautiful thing to watch this God-created horse run in real life. When an autopsy was done on him after his death, it was discovered that this huge chestnut stallion had a heart that was 2.5 times larger than the average!

## AN UNCOMMON PRAYER

The Psalmist prayed for an enlarged heart. He asked this for one reason: so he could better "run in the way of (God's) commandments." He wanted to run—hard, fast, long—after God. He longed to deeply pursue what God desired and communicated through His word. He wanted to finish his unique course and he prayed for the heart capacity to accomplish this spiritual feat.

Paul tells us in 1 Thessalonians 5:14 that we are to "encourage the faint-hearted." The phrase could be better translated "small-souled." Some people have diminutive souls—small minds, small emotions, small wills. Their "heart" capacity is below average and unable to deal strongly and fully with what God commands. They are weak and need extra care and encouragement and often don't run their race well.

The Psalmist prayed that God would increase his spiritual capacity, like Solomon in the early days of his life: "And God gave Solomon wisdom and understanding beyond measure, and breadth of mind like the sand on the seashore" (1 Kings 4:29).

## AN UNCOMMON HEART

Hearts like Secretariat's are made large by genetics and exercise. Human hearts, like the Psalmist's and Solomon's, are expanded by God's gracious intervention and spiritual exercise—by renewing the mind, surrendering the will, submitting the emotions. By listening to the Lord daily and responding instantly to the promptings of God's Spirit and the illumination of His Word. By spiritual discipline and passionate intention.

All of us begin our spiritual life with a depraved, sinful heart. Only God's work changes this from a heart of stone to a heart filled with the Divine. Some believers fail to cultivate their spiritual life. But there are many who become giants for God through intimacy and cooperation with Him.

Do you want to finish like Secretariat? Do you desire to glorify God by stretching out beautifully and accomplishing all He has designed for you? Then pray for an enlarged heart … *and run your race!*

# DAY 22

## HOW TO GET THE TWO THINGS YOU REALLY WANT

THERE ARE MANY things the serious-minded believer does not care about. Through years of walking with Christ, they have seen the futility of chasing the trinkets of this world. It's not that they're not tempted to desire worldly attractions, it's that something else is of greater value.

### KNOWING GOD

They want to know God; to be intimate with Him; to experience daily the power of the Essential Presence. And secondly, they long to hear from God—His directives and instructions for all of life—and be used by Him for His glory and the expansion of His kingdom.

A man who is narrowed to this lane is poised to win the race. If he is armed with the Spirit of God and the Word of God, he has the resources to face absolutely anything in the path. What more could he want? What more could he possibly need?

### IT COMES WITH A PRICE

God knows this is exactly what a man needs for fruitful, joyful kingdom living. And that is why, in the very first chapter of His most direct book of wisdom (Proverbs), He clearly tells us how to obtain these essentials. He goes so far as to promise a full supply of these things, but this promise is based upon one simple condition.

> *If you turn to my reproof, behold, I will pour out my Spirit on you; I will make my words known to you. (Proverbs 1:23)*

Any man can have the fullness of His Spirit and the illumination of His word—everything they need. The condition is simple: listen and respond.

"When I reprove you," God is saying, "then repent. Turn quickly. Honor Me enough and trust Me enough to believe that what I'm telling you is right and is the very best thing for your good and My glory. Then respond instantly to the promptings of My Spirit and the illumination of My word. If you will do this, I will give you the gifts you desire in full measure."

An inexhaustible supply is promised for everything we need. But it is conditioned by a simple request for obedience from the God who sees all and knows what's best for our lives.

## AND A WARNING

God further describes what happens to a man who refuses God's counsel and will not turn at His reproof. The results are disastrous for such a show of pride. This man will taste the self-inflicted wounds of a God-less life.

> *"So they shall eat of the fruit of their own way and be satiated with their own devices. For the waywardness of the naive will kill them, and the complacency of fools will destroy them. (Verses 31-32)*

We twist and turn and manipulate to get what we think we need. We look to a thousand different sources. But the path to what we desire is exceedingly simple, promised in 23 words for all to experience.

Has God given you a word of reproof lately? In light of what's at stake, why not turn right now?

## DAY 23

# THE MOST IMPORTANT IMAGE YOU WILL EVER SEE

AFTER JESUS ADDRESSED His churches in Revelation, Chapters 2-3, He took John into the holiest spot in heaven or earth. Here He reminded him (and us) of why we should adjust our lives and churches to God's agenda and live a life of absolute surrender to Him.

> *After these things I looked, and behold, a door standing open in heaven, and the first voice which I had heard, like the sound of a trumpet speaking with me, said, "Come up here, and I will show you what must take place after these things." Immediately I was in the Spirit; and behold, a throne was standing in heaven, and One sitting on the throne. (Revelation 4:1-2)*

### A DOOR STANDING OPEN IN HEAVEN

God is not hiding. He gave John the ability to step into the Holy of Holies and observe the most important. The first moment of this vision gave John the premier perspective and then he was led to record it so we could gain this perspective also. And now through the ages, the Spirit of God invites every new believer to see what is behind this door.

God does not hide Himself or His revelation of the future from John nor us. Of all of God's amazing attributes, one of the most precious is His self-disclosure—His willingness to be seen, known, and understood. Here is an open door. But, even further, here is ...

## THE THRONE AND ONE SEATED UPON IT

This one sentence explains everything and settles everything. There He is—always, eternally, constantly, perfectly, triumphantly. There are not two gods occupying this place, but One. God is seated upon the throne above every throne in heaven and earth. It is the place of ultimate authority.

When we see Him there we realize that everything comes from Him ("In the beginning, God created"); everything belongs to Him ("The earth is the Lord's and the fullness thereof"); everything is sovereignly overseen by Him ("His sovereignty rules over all"), and everything worships Him ("Every knee will bow and every tongue confess that Jesus Christ is Lord to the glory of God the Father"). The Throne corrects our proud hearts and scattered minds. This one vision explains it all and redeems it all.

## THE LONG LOOK

We must look deeply at the Throne. We should open the door and gaze humbly and often until this image burns into our spiritual retina. Only this vision will help us remember who we are and whose we are. Only here will we realize our ancient Enemy is a defeated foe beneath God's feet.

From this Throne we receive our marching orders and know that He is the only One we live to please. Only here are hearts relax in joyful rest, for all is well.

## DAY 24

# THE VOICE FROM THE MERCY SEAT

*Now when Moses went into the tent of meeting to speak with Him, he heard the voice speaking to him from above the mercy seat that was on the ark of the testimony, from between the two cherubim, so He spoke to him.*

*(Numbers 7:89)*

In our familiarity with the Scripture and our distance from the actual events, we can lose the magnitude of what the Bible is saying to us.

Pause and read the single verse above. In fact, read it several times and ask the Voice above the mercy seat to help you see what actually occurred. And then, read it again and again, asking Him what this means for you.

Let this one verse of Spirit-breathed Scripture, active and alive, explode in your understanding. Hear His voice to you behind the printed words.

## We can approach God!

"Moses went into the tent of meeting to speak with Him" the Bible tells us. Why was the tabernacle also called the tent of meeting? It was not a gathering place with the whole congregation. It was an intimate meeting place between God and man.

It was clear that Moses went to this place for that solitary purpose: "to speak with Him." Think of this. Since the Garden, God has made it possible for us to walk with Him in the cool of the day and commune with Him.

All through the Old Testament record we see this continual exchange between God and man. Abraham heard God's voice, as did Moses, and Joshua, and David; Elijah and Elisha and all the prophets.

A young teenager named Mary and her finance, Joseph, both heard Him, as did Peter and later, Paul. All the way to John in the book that is named for such communion (the Revelation) which says to us, "Hear what the Spirit is *saying* [present tense] to the churches."

Scan the whole counsel of Scripture and realize it is a running record of communication. God speaks, and we can hear Him! And in His voice, we hear all we need for direction, comfort, encouragement, life, and light.

## AT THE MERCY SEAT

It is no accident that Moses was directed to the one place where this communication was possible. The mercy seat represented the action that was required for us to approach God. It was a place that spoke of the great Sacrifice that would provide for our continual communion. And a place where God would extend His grace for us to approach Him.

Later, the writer of Hebrews would remind us of our Great High Priest who bids us "draw near with confidence to the throne of grace, so that we may receive mercy and find grace to help in time of need" (Hebrews 4:16).

This should humble us. We do not come in arrogance, but in quiet confidence in Christ's atonement for our sin and His gracious invitation for us to approach our Father. We have been introduced by the slain Lamb into this "grace in which we now stand," where we have peace facing God (Romans 5:1). We can enter now into the tent of meeting and hear His voice. We are even invited to come and pray without ceasing.

## AND WAIT FOR HIS VOICE

Later in this account we see Moses, as others come to him for direction, making these kinds of statements: "Wait, and I will *listen* to what the Lord will *command* concerning you." Then the Lord *spoke* to Moses, *saying* ..." (Numbers 9:8-9).

This is a picture of our posture. We are to approach and listen. We are to wait on Him and move only at His initiation and instruction. We are to hear Him and be careful, like Joshua, to do all that He says, not turning to the left or to the right from His instruction.

If He finds us listening, we will find Him speaking. And then we will have the glorious privilege of being led by the Great Shepherd of the sheep. The Lion of the tribe of Judah will go before us. We will prosper because we are led by the

One-Who-Sees. We will hear a Voice behind us saying "This is the way; walk in it."

And the sacred transaction between man and God will occur once again.

# DAY 25

## RECOGNIZING THE MESSIAH

WHY IS IT that some people see what others do not? That there are people who recognize God and His activity while those right next to them are completely oblivious?

### A LONG LOOK IN THE RIGHT DIRECTION

Anna was a widow in Jerusalem during the birth of Christ. The Bible says she "never left the temple, serving night and day with fastings and prayers" (Luke 2:36). She had been doing this for many, many years.

Think of it this way: she had positioned herself in the environments of God's presence, seeking the Messiah. She had continually fasted and prayed, both signs of intense pursuit and spiritual discipline that God rewards.

People who are not interested in finding and hearing God do not do these things. But those who are intensely interested in Christ regularly fast and pray, not to appease God, but to pursue Him.

When the 8-day-old baby Jesus was brought into the temple, others merely saw another Jewish boy. Anna saw Christ. And "at that very moment she came up and began giving thanks to God, and continued to speak of Him to all those who were looking for the redemption of Jerusalem" (Luke 2:38). When you see Him, it is so wonderful and rewarding, you cannot help but tell others.

## EYES TO SEE

Anna had a heart that was ready to believe. When the real Christ came into the room, she knew it. Instantly. Do you?

Are your spiritual antennae up? Do you fast and pray in pursuit of Christ? Just to "know Him," as Paul said? Is there a drive in you that outweighs the drive for pleasure, comfort, recognition and fame? For any and every other pursuit except Him?

Millions ignore Christ's obvious presence. They miss the most important thing in heaven and earth and suffer eternally with the loss.

But if you seek Him—earnestly and continually—you will be one of the privileged on earth. For God rewards those who pursue Him with the greatest gift of all. You will find Him ... and you will have everything.

## DAY 26

# THE CURSE OF A DIVIDED LOVE

THE DILEMMA OF our lives, evident since the fall, is the tragedy of a divided love. Every problem in our lives (and in our world) would be solved if we simply followed the first and foremost commandment: to love God with no divisions.

> *One of the scribes came and heard them arguing, and recognizing that He had answered them well, asked Him, "What commandment is the foremost of all?" Jesus answered, "The foremost is, 'Hear, O Israel! The Lord our God is one Lord; and you shall love the Lord your God with all your heart, and with all your soul, and with all your mind, and with all your strength.' The second is this, 'You shall love your neighbor as yourself.' There is no other commandment greater than these." (Mark 12:28-31)*

## ALL

Notice the four uses of "all" in this command: "*all* your heart ... *all* your soul ... *all* your mind ... *all* your strength." Most of us know little of such unified devotion. It is easy to divide our affections, our souls (mind, emotion, and will), and our strength between multiple pursuits. We are "half-hearted creatures" as C.S. Lewis says, playing around with the things of this world and missing what an undivided love could bring to us.

## ALL IS POSSIBLE

But there is something vital we must consider. Jesus said, "You *shall* love ..." like this. If God is God, then He cannot ask us to do anything that we cannot do by His grace. If He tells us to forgive, then we can forgive. To pray without ceasing, then it is possible. And here He tells us to love Him wholly with every fiber of our heart, soul, mind, and strength. This means it is not only commanded, it is possible. This should be the normal Christian experience.

## BEGIN WITH A TEST

Exams are designed to help us see where we really are. To begin this process, we must start with a brutally honest self-examination. What do we love? When you love something, you pursue it, cherish it, give time and attention to it, live for it.

So, what object in our lives garners that kind of attention? Ourselves? Do we protect, cherish, and pursue everything we can for ourselves? Then we love self more than Him, for instance. Do we pursue, cherish, give time and attention, and live for our reputation? Our comfort? Our pleasure?

And if there is anything else in Christ's place, what is it? What has pulled us away from simple, pure devotion to Jesus Christ?

## LESS-THAN-ALL IS IDOLATRY

Whatever has become the object of our deep affection has become our god—the thing we worship. And we are to have "no other gods" beside Him. The great "Shema" has been written on the doorpost of every Jewish home for centuries and should be inscribed on the entry to our lives. "The Lord our God, the Lord is one." There is One God, He is OUR God, and He is to be our Lord and Master. No one else should be worshiped or served.

## "ALL" LEADS TO FULFILLMENT OF ALL THAT MATTERS AND LASTS

Not only are these "all's" commanded, but their observance is the key to the fulfillment of the greatest horizontal command—to "love your neighbor as yourself." Isn't this what heaven is like? A "world of love" as Jonathan Edwards describes? Paul would later say that "Love does no wrong to a neighbor; therefore, love is the fulfillment of the law" (Romans 13:10). When you are in this flow of vertical and horizontal love you will fulfill every command because you will be driven by the greatest force and purest motivation.

It would seem our highest goal today would be to love Him like this. Refuse every other affection that is placed above Him. Evaluate every Siren call from the enemy as a deadly temptation, pulling you away from the greatest, most important command. Refuse to "love the world and the things of the world" which are temporal, fleeting, and only momentarily fulfilling.

At the end of the day it boils down to the one question Jesus asked of Peter and of us: "Do you love Me more than these?"

Well, do you?

# DAY 27

## Selective Hearing

Raising kids is a great privilege and, most of the time, an incredible joy. But there is a congenital defect that runs through every household, creating tension and causing conflict: the selective hearing of children.

It's amazing. Here's a child with perfect ears. In fact, you don't have to take him to an audiologist to test his hearing. Just go in a closet as far away from him as possible and whisper, "Let's go get some ice cream" and he bounds down the stairs from the second story with his shoes on, ready to go.

But stand over him as he's watching television and shout in his ear, "Take out the garbage, son," and he's stone deaf. At least, that's what he tells you an hour later when you return and the garbage is still there. "I didn't hear you, Dad." Stunning. Of course, they come by it honest—sons learn this from their dads as they observe it in operation with their wives!

We're good at this. The tragedy is that it transfers to our relationship with the Voice that really matters. We don't really listen to Jesus.

### Why Aren't You Hearing?

The Pharisees had a man who had been blind from birth standing right in front of them. Jesus had healed him.

The most unobservant person in Jerusalem would easily agree. But the well-taught Pharisees would not accept this explanation. As they questioned the miraculously healed man over and over again, in desperation he finally cried out:

> *"I have told you already, and you would not listen. Why do you want to hear it again?" (John 9:27)*

The tragedy was, the sounds were reaching their ears, the signal was registering in their physical brains, but their hearts refused to hear the truth. Soul hearing is what God describes as full hearing.

If they had just listened—really listened—their eyes would have been opened just like the blind man. But their preconceived ideas of reality and their incredible pride closed their ears to the truth.

## HE WHO HAS EARS TO HEAR

In the letters to the seven churches in the Revelation, Jesus speaks to each church, telling them what they must do or their lampstand would be removed. He closes every letter with these words: "He who has ears to hear, let him hear." He's speaking. It would be wise to pay attention and obey. Everything depends upon our hearing.

Spiritual hearing happens through hunger, willingness, and surrender. When those components are present in a conversation with Christ, the truth is amazingly clear, even when Jesus speaks in a still, small voice. But if there is pride, unwillingness, and determined rebellion, He can stand over us and shout, but we will not hear the essential Voice.

## DAY 28

# THE MOST DISASTROUS WORD

*"Go up to a land flowing with milk and honey; for I will not go up in your midst, because you are an obstinate people, and I might destroy you on the way." When the people heard this sad word, they went into mourning, and none of them put on his ornaments.*

*(Exodus 33:3-4)*

There is one thing and one thing alone that makes a follower of Christ distinctive. One thing that provides what is needed. One thing that carries us. One thing that gives power and needed provision.

Everything flows from the presence of the Lord. Everything. When you have Him—and have Him fully—you have everything you need. When His presence is lifted from your life you are nothing more than a sinful mortal with only the limited resources that affords. This is why Jesus said, "Apart from Me, you can do nothing" (John 15:4-5).

## THE LOSS

God's manifest presence is not always guaranteed. For a believer, God has promised that He will "never leave us nor forsake us." He is there in the life of His children, even when we are sinful, doing things for us that we don't even realize. When we are faithless, He still remains faithful.

But the blatant turn to worship other idols, as the Israelites did in the passage above, can cause us to lose the fullness of His presence. God will not participate in such nonsense.

What true Christian has not felt such a spiritual vacuum? The loss of intimacy that causes us to hear the most disastrous word: "I will not go up with you"?

## THE RETURN

Moses response to this announcement from God was swift and sure. He interceded with God. In humility Moses admitted his and the people's sin, but pled for God's full return. He based this on God's promises and His glory. "Consider too that this nation is your people," Moses prayed (Exodus 33:13).

God longs to display Himself. He loves His children. He loves the world and knows that what we all need is Him. And, He is waiting for us to draw near to Him and has promised in return to draw near to us. This is the price we must pay for continued intimacy with Him.

Have you heard the disastrous word? If so, then run to Him. Plead with Him on the basis of His glory, promises, and purposes. Do anything He asks to restore the intimacy of His presence. Pray the prayer of Moses ...

> *The he said to Him, "If Your presence does not go with us, do not lead us up from here. For how then can it be known that I have found favor in Your sight, I and Your people? Is it not by Your going with us, so that we, I and Your people, may be distinguished from all the other people who are upon the face of the earth?" (Exodus 33:15-16)*

Do not stop until you hear His gracious words: "My presence will go with you" (Exodus 33:14). Because, everything of value flows from the presence of the Lord. Everything.

## DAY 29

# THE STRUGGLE THAT DESTROYS AND REMAKES US

*"I have seen God face to face*
*and yet my life has been delivered."*

*(Genesis 32:30)*

It is doubtful that any man will be changed into Christ's likeness without moments of intense battle. The flesh dies hard.

In God's infinite jealousy for His chosen children, He boxes us in by simply letting us have our own way. He knows that, given enough rope, we will hang ourselves and only when the noose is around our neck will we be ready to turn to Him in brokenness and genuine repentance. A. W. Tozer was right: "It is doubtful if God can use a man greatly unless He hurts him deeply."

## THE JACOB SYNDROME

We are like Jacob. He was an independent, devious man. All his life he had known something of God, but not enough. He had known God through his heritage but not his experience. In His mercy, God had protected Jacob enough so that he would not destroy himself, but let him loose enough to bring him to a Jabbok moment.

One lonely night, Jacob found himself with his angry father-in-law behind him and his estranged brother, Esau, in front of him. He was hemmed in by the consequences of his own ways. This is where his self-life had placed him and it was a frightful spot, alone by the Jabbok river. In the darkness of the night, Jacob was feeling the crushing weight of his own choices as God was deliberately bringing him to the end of himself.

## THE JABBOK ENCOUNTER

At this precise moment, he encountered God and it was not pleasant. We will only discover the nature of this struggle in eternity, but it was described as "wrestling." All night long, Jacob and the Lord fought with each other. As the morning dawned, Jacob's Divine opponent had "not prevailed against him" and so "He touched the socket of his thigh; so the socket of Jacob's thigh was dislocated while he wrestled with him" (Genesis 32:25). God gave the necessary, disabling blow.

Finally, the limping wrestler realized that God and God alone was the Source. No one else could save him. None but God could bless him and he cried out for God.

This was the point of the exercise. Now God was free to give the ultimate blessing: He changed Jacob and sealed this transformation by the bestowing of a new name. The sinful Jacob became the devout Israel and was now ready to walk into the fullness of his destiny.

## THE PENIEL ALTAR

Now, like his father and grandfather before Him, the knowing Israel could build an altar of true worship. He was no longer a spectator but a willing participant in God's redemptive history.

> *The great preacher Martyn Lloyd-Jones was once asked, "What does a person look like who has truly met God?" Alluding to Genesis 32:31, he replied, "He walks with a limp." … After encountering the living Christ, Jacob was forever crippled—both physically and in regard to his ego. He could no longer strut around arrogantly as he had done before. His pride turned to lowliness (33:3). His greed turned to generosity (33:10–11). And his self-reliance had turned into worship (33:20). So, we who are professing believers must ask ourselves: Have these things happened to me? Have my habits changed? Have I met the Lord?* (Strassner, "Opening Up Genesis")

If you have not come to the Jabbok you may still vainly believe that your plans will work, your strength is sufficient, and your wisdom is impeccable. If you sense that may be so, cry out for the Lord to take you to the river.

It may be that only a lonely night at the Jabbok and a sweaty striving with your Master will work this out of you. It may be a frightful night, but it will hurt you in the best possible way.

## DAY 30

# THE ENCOUNTER THAT CHANGES EVERYTHING

It is remarkable that God makes Himself known. He doesn't have to reveal Himself and there is nothing inside of Him that needs us. But in His sovereign plan, He has chosen to build a nation of people who can know Him and be known by Him.

## THE INVITATION

This self-disclosure always begins with an invitation, such as God gave to Moses.

> *The Lord said to Moses, "Come up to me on the mountain and wait there, that I may give you the tablets of stone, with the law and the commandment, which I have written for their instruction." (Exodus 24:12)*

Moses had encountered God and knew His voice. He had been invited by God to turn aside to a burning bush once when he was tending sheep in the wilderness on the west side of Mount Sinai. This Divine Encounter set him on a course to help deliver an entire nation. Sometime later, as

Moses comes to the same mountain, now with several million Israelites in tow, the Lord invites him to turn aside.

Little did Moses know this simple invitation would lead to an encounter that changed history. Moses had no idea how catalytic that moment would be.

## THE CHOICE

With God's invitation, there is always a choice. Moses could have walked away, fearful or uninterested. He could have responded with a selfish "what's-in-it-for-me?" He could have reasoned that the demands of leading an entire nation left him no time to wait on an unseen God.

There were hundreds of other voices calling for his attention. Moses had listened to those before, but 40 years in the wilderness has brought him to the settled conviction that one Voice always deserved an instant response.

> *So, Moses rose with his assistant Joshua, and Moses went up into the mountain of God. (Exodus 24:13)*

Perhaps Moses thought of his ancestor, Abraham, who was called to take his son and sacrifice young Isaac on Mount Moriah. The Bible records no hesitation but simply that he "arose and went" and the results were life-changing.

Now Moses does the same. Without a word of doubt or fear Moses quickly turns aside to wait expectantly for his Commander-in-Chief.

This encounter changed everything—for Moses, for God's people, for human history. Four thousand years later, that exchange and the Ten Commandments given still reveal the nature of God and show us our need for a Savior. The words Moses received continue to be a tutor that leads us to Christ. And coming to Christ, we can now receive the Presence that enables us to rise to those commandments.

God is still writing His-story. Who knows but what God's invitation to you to "come up to me on the mountain and wait there" will not have similar consequences for you and others.

# DAY 31

## THE DECISION IS YOURS

*Only one thing is necessary.*
*Mary has chosen the good part*
*which shall not be taken away from her.*

(LUKE 10:42)

THERE IS NOTHING more valuable than intimacy with Christ. Everything in life rises and falls on staying near to Christ—walking, listening, obeying, loving Him. So why do we often find ourselves pulled away from the place of such treasures?

### INTIMACY IS OFTEN LOST THROUGH THE LURE OF MANY GOOD THINGS

A myriad of voices pull us away from the simplicity and purity of devotion to Jesus Christ. Just ask Martha (Luke 10:38-42). Busy about many good things, she missed the essential thing. Jesus revealed to her the results of a distracted life. Evaluate your life with this four-point test and see if you are related to Martha. (Circle each one that applies.)

- **Are you WORRIED?** *"Martha, you are worried … about so many things." (Verse 41)*
- **Are you FRUSTRATED?** *"Martha, you are … bothered" (Verse 41)*
- **Are you ANGRY and DEMANDING?** *"Lord, do you not care that my sister has left me to do all the serving alone? Then tell her to help me!" (Verse 40)*
- **Are you WHINING?** *(see the verse above and imagine the tone of her self-pitying voice as she complains to Christ!)*

Each of the above are clear signs that we have been drawn away and lost that which is most fundamental to our souls. For many, we fail to see the inestimable value of closeness with Him.

## INTIMACY IS THE SOLE PORTAL TO WHAT MATTERS AND LASTS

The World-Wide-Web is amazing. Upon entrance, you will find trillions of bytes of information regarding every conceivable topic. But you must enter a portal. If you do not, all that is behind the door is unattainable.

Intimacy with Christ is the portal that gives you access to everything of value. When Jesus spoke of Mary's choice of "(sitting) at the Lord's feet, listening to His Word," He said that, "Mary has chosen the good part which will not be taken away from her" (Verse 39, 42).

Intimacy brings us **RELATIONSHIP**. Even if you lose men's applause, intimacy gives you ultimate approval and love.

Only through intimacy do we find **REALITY.** Even if circumstances cloud and confuse, intimacy gives you perfect perspective from the One who sees the end from the beginning.

The path to **ADVENTURE** begins in Christ's presence. Even if life binds and confines you, intimacy restores your passion and calling from the One who knows your true heart.

When life is just not right, time with Christ brings **ALIGNMENT**. Even if the world, flesh, and devil sidetrack you, intimacy draws you back to live for God's glory.

And without God's presence, you have no hope of **EFFECTIVENESS**. Even if you are weak, intimacy unleashes the God of the universe through you!

## INTIMACY COMES THROUGH AN INVITATION AND A CHOICE

It is mind-boggling that Christ invites us to come and be with him—but He does!

> *Come, all you who are weary and heavy-laden, and I will give you rest. (Matthew 11:28)*

> *Let all who are thirsty come and drink of the water of life freely and without cost. (Revelation 22:17)*

> *If any man is thirsty, let him come unto Me and drink (John 7:37)*

Mary made that choice. Refusing to be distracted, she chose to sit in the presence of the Shepherd and Guardian of her soul. She bent to the right posture in humility at His feet and the right action—listening to the Lord's word. Our first response to Christ's presence should be silence and an attentive heart.

J. Oswald Sanders in his classic book, "Enjoying Intimacy with God" reminds us of the way of access.

> *Each of the disciples was as close to Jesus as he chose to be for the Son of God had no favorites. With him there is no caprice of favoritism. Their relationship with Him was the result of their own choice, conscious or unconscious. It is a sobering thought that we too are as close to Christ as we really choose to be.*
>
> *It would seem that admission to the inner circle of deepening intimacy with God is the outcome of deep desire. Only those who count such intimacy a prize worth sacrificing anything else for, are likely to attain it. If other intimacies are more desirable to us, we will not gain entry to that circle.*
>
> *The place on Jesus' breast is still vacant and open to any who are willing to pay the price of deepening intimacy. We are now and we will be in the future only as intimate with God as we really choose to be.*

## DAY 32

# DO YOU WANT TO LIVE A REVIVED LIFE TODAY?

IF THERE EVER was a man who knew how to live, it was Paul. He seized the most of every moment and came with satisfaction to the end of his life saying, "I have finished my course, I have fought the good fight, I have kept the faith" (2 Timothy 4:7).

I'd love to walk into heaven with that statement on my lips. And I'd love to come to the end of *today* with that same contentment. In fact, as leaders, we must walk like this, for our greatest leadership comes from the undeniable example of a revived life.

So how do we really live? Listen to Paul's prescription:

> *So then, brothers, we are debtors, not to the flesh, to live according to the flesh. For if you live according to the flesh you will die, but if by the Spirit you put to death the deeds of the body, you will live. For all who are led by the Spirit of God are sons of God. (Romans 8:12-14)*

Paul is explaining who we are in Christ. He contrasts "flesh" men (those who only have themselves, but no Christ) with "Spirit" men (those who now have the Spirit living in them and all the resources He affords). This mystical infusion of God into us, made possible by nothing less than grace, has made us debtors. We have something we don't deserve, rendering us accountable for a right response. To whom much is given, much is required.

## OUR PHYSICAL BODIES

... simply respond to stimuli and are amoral. If we are out in the winter air, our bodies feel cold. If we touch a hot stove, we feel pain. If we have the emotion of anger from within and the mental stupidity to do it, we can influence our bodies to shout at our mate. The body is merely a tool.

For a believer, the Spirit of God now lives within us. The engine is now in the car. We have a greater power to influence our bodies and souls in a new direction.

## NOW WE MUST LIVE

... from the inside out. But this requires a continual choice. We must defer to Him. For years we have been living at the influence of our own mind, the impulses of our own emotions, and the impetus of our own will. Now, there is a new Master in town. The Spirit of God lives in us. We must renew our minds through His Word, submit our emotions to His control, and surrender our will to His will on every occasion.

When we are living in glad submission to the Spirit, He will not only prompt us, but empower us. Now, our body is the servant of this King and will respond accordingly. As long as our soul remains submissive to the Spirit and allows God within to give direction, we will "put to death the (sinful) deeds of the body." We are now being "led by the Spirit."

## THE HAPPY RESULT

... of this dependency is life. Life as it was intended. Life that is good and right. Life that is holy and influential. Life that is effective and fulfilling. Life as God designed. It is, in fact, the life of none other than God, living through our mortal flesh. And this life illustrates that we are sons and daughters of God.

## DAY 33

# THE DETERMINATION THAT PRODUCES INTIMACY

*"And rising very early in the morning, while it was still dark, he departed and went out to a desolate place, and there he prayed."*

*(Mark 1:35)*

There are some people who carry the sweet aroma of God about them. It is evident they have been with the Father and when you are around them it feels like they know things others do not know and see things others cannot see.

Why is it that these people experience greater intimacy with their Father than others? There are reasons and we see this clearly in a simple statement about the life of the man, Jesus Christ. Notice the four verbs in this verse that speak of Jesus' determination, as a man, to connect with God.

### "RISING"

Jesus got up "very early in the morning while it was till dark." How many men or women miss the moment with God simply because they will not rise? When God prompts their heart to experience solitude and communion with him, they love their flesh more than intimacy with the Father.

"A little sleep, a little slumber, a little folding of the hands to rest and your poverty will come in like a flood and your need like an armed man" (Proverbs 6:10). The love of comfort can abort intimacy with God.

## "DEPARTED"

Jesus was willing to leave the comfort and security of the crowd. Everyone was looking for him, His Apostles later said, but Jesus considered time with His Father more important than time with men. If you are never inaccessible you usually have nothing to say when you are accessible. Jesus knew that everything depended on his communion with the Father and therefore he was willing to leave the familiar, the comfortable, the safe, the crowd.

## "WENT OUT"

Geography is important. Jesus retired to a "desolate place," knowing there is something crucial about solitude. We can hear God in the midst, of course, but there is an importance in a quiet place. Jesus went to a location where there was no noise. He altered His environment to gain a greater capacity to hear. Mark Batterson was quoted as saying, "Change of place + change of pace = change of perspective."

Like the Psalmist, Jesus composed and quieted his soul. Retreating from competing voices so we can hear the still, small voice of God should be our daily experience.

## "PRAYED"

"And there he prayed." Jesus could have prayed—and did pray—everywhere. But it says of this spot that "*there*" he prayed. He was going somewhere, moving in a direction with a deliberate purpose. He made time for this. It was a distinct choice and he utilized the time when he arrived. "There He prayed."

Jesus knew that this was His lifeline—that everything depended on His communion with the Source of life, direction, wisdom, and power. He valued prayer so much that it took priority over fellowship with others or the comfort of an early morning bed.

For many, this moment might have read "and there he thought" or "and there he checked his messages" or "and there he worked." But not Jesus. The business of solitude was singular. *"And there he prayed."*

## DAY 34

# THE DELIBERATE, CONSTANT CHOICE OF A COMPOSED, QUIETED SOUL

LIFE IS FILLED with overwhelming noise. Our old and constant Enemy orchestrates a cacophony of confusion around us. If we are not careful, we will fall right into his trap and the results are disastrous.

The secret of David's spiritual success was his determined choice to quiet his soul, explained to us in three short verses that compose Psalm 131.

> *O Lord, my heart is not proud, nor my eyes haughty; nor do I involve myself in great matters, or in things too difficult for me. Surely I have composed and quieted my soul. Like a weaned child rests against his mother, my soul is like a weaned child within me. O Israel, hope in the Lord from this time forth and forever.*

David knew his limitations. Years on the Judean hillside had taught him the absolute necessity of a quieted soul that found not only God's comfort, but direction. Therefore, when thrust into the limelight of national politics, he chose to humbly do what he could about the matters around him without the neglect of intimacy with the Master. To lose this, was to lose the one Voice that could sustain and direct him.

## BE STILL MY SOUL

Our soul is composed of our **mind** (where we think), our **emotions** (where we feel), and our **will** (where we decide). Before the Spirit indwells us, our soul is our only operating system. Our human spirit is dead because it has not yet been regenerated by the Spirit of God. Salvation remedies this lack.

If we are not careful, we will revert to these soulish faculties after salvation instead of listening to the Spirit and following His leadership. An untamed soul can pull us in a thousand directions and create so much noise that the still, small voice of the Lord is undiscernible.

The serious follower of Christ must continually **renew** his mind, **tame** his emotions, and **surrender** his will to the will of God. This is possible through God's grace and the power of the indwelling Spirit. But without the believer's conscious and determined choice to do so, he will naturally slide into a busied, soulish life. The Spirit within will be muted and life will be driven by humanism.

## A WEANED CHILD

The results are stunning for those who daily, deliberately refuse the noise. Who take time throughout the day to humbly admit their need and quiet their soul with a hunger to hear.

David said that, "Like a weaned child rests against his mother, my soul is like a weaned child within me." A weaned child has left his mother's breast, but only recently. He intuitively still longs for the closeness and comfort, the emotional and physical nourishment that this intimacy provided. He still wants to lean in.

The Psalmist's mind, emotions, and will were pressing in to encounter Christ—to listen to His heartbeat, to feel His warmth and affection, to receive His direction.

"Draw near to Christ, and He will draw near to you," James promises. Without Him, we will find ourselves starving from a lack of affection which only His presence provides.

# DAY 35

## KNOWING GOD

"GOD IS EASY to live with," Tozer said. Part of this ease is because of God's willingness to be understood. His self-disclosure. He is waiting to be known.

If you don't want a relationship with someone, you go dark. You are unwilling to be transparent. God's self-disclosure indicates His invitation to intimacy. And here is the greatest delight, for "In His presence is fullness of joy and at His right hand are pleasures forevermore" (Psalm 16:11).

And so, David, who know God well, reminds us in his prayer of the path to intimacy with the Father.

> *"Make me know Your ways, O Lord; teach me Your paths. Lead me in Your truth and teach me, for you are the God of my salvation. For you I wait all the day." (Psalms 25:4-5)*

### HIS WAYS

Everyone has their ways. "He always does that," we say of a friend, "It's just his way." Our ways describe what we value and how we operate. They display our character and determination.

God has His ways and He has made them known. So, David asks God for a great favor: "Make me know Your ways, O Lord." He wanted to know God and He knew He could come to know Him more by knowing His ways.

*Are you a student of the ways of God?*

## HIS PATHS

God has paths for us, and they all lead to an increasing knowledge of Him. We can resist His paths. We can choose the broad path that leads to destruction, or determine that we will increasingly choose the narrow path that leads to Him.

Christ walks on this path with us. To walk His paths is to know Him more, like the two who walked with Him on the road to Emmaus and declared, "Did not our hearts burn within us as we walked with Him along the way?"

*Are you walking on His paths? You will not grow in intimacy if you are unwilling to follow Him.*

## HIS TRUTH

God has most deeply displayed Himself through His Word, and His word is truth. In pen and ink, in 66 books over 1500 years, through God-breathed inspiration, God has laid down His description of Himself. His Word leads us to not merely know the truth—but to know Him. J.C. MacCauley penned this beautifully:

*I read Thy Word, O Lord, each passing day,*
*And in Thy sacred page find glad employ.*
*But this I pray:*
*Save from the killing letter.*
*Teach my heart, set free from human forms,*
*The holy art of reading Thee in every line,*
*In precept, prophecy, and sign.*
*Till all my vision filled with Thee,*
*Thy likeness shall reflect in me.*
*Not knowledge, but Thyself my joy!*
*For this I pray.*

*Are you reading God's Word daily? He is there on every page. Are you reading the Bible to encounter Him?*

## TO KNOW HIM

David knew that the secret to life was to intimately and experientially know God and so he "waited" on the Lord. To wait is to stand at attention—looking towards God in eager anticipation.

Paul would later confirm this value. "I count all things but loss for the surpassing value of knowing Christ Jesus my Lord" (Philippians 3:8).

God is waiting to disclose Himself to you and has done everything to make this possible. If we don't experience Him it is our own fault.

*Are you waiting on Him? Aggressively learning His ways, faithfully walking His path, and fervently studying His Word so that you may know Him?*

**DAY 36**

# THE LOVINGKINDNESS OF OUR GREAT GOD

THE GREAT LIAR is relentless in his assault upon the One whose throne he longs to dispossess. We were designed to praise God—to give Him glory in the highest order. To abort that, Satan wages a relentless assault in our thinking as to the character of God.

"God is not loving and He certainly is not kind," he whispers at every dark moment in our experience. "If he loved you, He would not have allowed this to happen."

He never misses an opportunity to defame God.

## IF WE ARE NOT WISE

... we will fail to recognize the source of these thoughts. A creeping mistrust will slide in like a morning fog over our hearts. Doubts will arise as to God's goodness and we will find ourselves unwilling to surrender to this God we now question. (Why would we give ourselves to One we do not think has our best interest at heart?)

But this is the purpose of the Bible. It records for all time the truth about God, the hidden agenda behind all His ways. It stands by our favorite chair, like a sentinel; waiting at every moment to defend the Father. To speak the truth about the lovingkindness of our God.

The Spirit whispers to us to open its pages and see the testimony of millions who have discovered the truth about the Father. It beckons us to sink in surrender into His arms.

David saw it and it repeatedly strengthened his soul and corrected his steps in the midst of the darkness.

> *"Because of [my enemy's] strength I will watch for You, for God is my stronghold. My God in His lovingkindness will meet me; God will let me look triumphantly upon my foes ... But as for me, I shall sing of Your strength. Yes, I will joyfully sing of Your lovingkindness in the morning, for You have been my stronghold and a refuge in the day of my distress. O my strength, I will sing praises to You, for God is my stronghold, the God who shows me lovingkindness." (Psalm 59:9-10, 16-17)*

Perhaps you're reading this right now because God wants you to recognize the whispers of the Enemy and the unchanging truth of God. Be wise. Recognize the Source of every doubt you feel rising in your soul. Resist the Enemy and he will flee from you.

And relax in God's goodness. He is not only loving in all His works toward You, He is exceedingly, perfectly, and eternally kind.

# DAY 37

## FINDING GOD

*Therefore, let everyone who is godly pray to*
*You in a time when You may be found;*
*surely in a flood of great waters*
*they will not reach Him.*

*(Psalm 32:6)*

God has gone to extraordinary lengths to make Himself accessible to us. Intimacy with God is readily available and He is no respecter of persons. If you seek Him, you will find Him, if you search for Him with all your heart.

But there are many who do not experience God on a *daily* basis. And, in times of crisis they find it hard to lay hold of God ... to find Him when they need Him most.

### Cultivated Intimacy

There are some people we know that are mere acquaintances. When we are in trouble, we don't generally turn to them. We don't have their contact information. We're not even sure we could get them if we tried. This is because we have not taken the steps necessary to develop a deep, intimate friendship.

It is possible for us to ignore God in the common day. We can fail to pay the necessary price of time and intentionality to build friendship with Him. It is not that God is not available. It is that the things of the world pull our minds and hearts away, and we see them as more valuable. Christ may be a reality to us, but a distant one.

## WHO DO YOU CALL?

Many are not quite sure how to access the Lord in a moment of difficulty. This puts them, not only in trouble, but without the One who can give them all they need in the middle of their dilemma.

Those who seek the Lord daily and have cultivated the art of intimacy with Him, know immediately where to go and how to lay hold of God. They understand the ways of God. They know how to access His promises. They have a long history of conversations that has left a rich deposit of truth imbedded in their hearts. They understand the posture of faith. They are patient and trusting because they have deeply experienced His goodness and understand His sovereignty. They know how to abide in Christ and how to bear remaining fruit.

If you want God in the future, you must seek Him in the present. And finding Him—both then and now—is what makes all the difference.

## DAY 38

# The Reason Your Day Is Not Going So Well

*And the four living creatures, each one of them having six wings, are full of eyes around and within; and day and night they do not cease to say, "Holy, holy, holy is the Lord God, the Almighty, who was and who is and who is to come."*

*(Revelation 4:8)*

It makes perfect sense that what is going on in heaven should be our constant aspiration. Heaven is where things are as they should be. This is why Christ told us that we should constantly pray, "Thy kingdom come, Thy will be done on earth as it [is being done] in heaven." We should be looking into the heavens for our direction in prayer and our pattern for living.

So, notice, at the beginning of this day, six telling words of heaven:

***... they do not cease to say***

Following those six words is one of the most profound statements recorded in human history. Angels proclaim God's holiness, power, and eternal existence. They remind us that He is different than anything and anyone; that He is the ALL mighty, (there is none greater), and that He has always been this way and always will be.

## OUR NEARSIGHTEDNESS

We forget this, or fail to see it altogether. And that is our problem.

We forget His holiness, and treat Him as any other created being. This leads to a lack of worship. We become too casual with God, or, worse yet, we ignore Him.

We forget His omnipotence. Which leads to a lack of dependency. We think we are mighty. This is why we resist God's control in our lives and find ourselves going through whole days living on our own without relying on God. Our prayerlessness is an indication of this. If we can go through a day with little or no prayer, it is a clear indication we think we can live our lives without God.

And we forget His eternal nature. No one is like our God. The Alpha and Omega. We should be looking to Him constantly for life and wisdom, understanding that His eternal nature gives Him something we do not have.

We forget, and move through our day with little or no remembrance of these essential truths. How else could we possibly explain our inattention to God on a daily basis?

## THE ACTIVITY OF HEAVEN

In heaven, there are special creatures who remind everyone of this day and night. They do not cease to remember and proclaim this glorious reality.

And, if we are to live rightly, we must join them. We must move to that unceasing recognition and unceasing worship. We must "not cease to say" these truths about God. This should be the foundation and framework for every thought, every relationship, and every decision of every day.

The more we live this way, the more heaven moves to earth … and the world around us sees the essence of our holy, almighty, eternal God.

## DAY 39

# WALKING WITH GOD

*"Noah was a righteous man, blameless in his time; Noah walked with God."*

*(Genesis 6:9)*

IT IS RARE. But in every generation, there are men and women who walk with God. They are the exceptions, because "broad is the road that leads to destruction and many are those who find it; and narrow is the road that leads to life, and few are those who find it."

But there are some who choose to walk with Jesus. And you can be counted among them. "God shows no caprice or favoritism," J. Oswald Sanders said. "You are as close to God as you really choose to be."

But what does such a life entail?

## WALKING

... implies movement. It is not stagnant. It indicates that something happens continually and daily. It is not a momentary experience, but an habitual lifestyle. Noah was not perfect in his walk, but it must have been the common experience of Noah to be following the movement and activity of God.

To walk means that you must stay up. You cannot lag behind in disobedience, or turn away in rebellion, or sit down in bitterness or unbelief. Walking requires the moment-by-moment decision to go where God is going, wherever and whenever God moves. A deliberate, continual choice to believe in God's will and follow His prompting.

You cannot follow your own agenda and walk with God. You do not make your own decisions as to direction, for your *singular* decision is to accept His direction. Jesus defined it in two words: "Follow Me."

## WITH GOD

But this walk is not with just anyone. If you are married, you walk with your wife through the course of your marriage. A child walks with his parents. Business associates walk with each other in their work life.

But Noah walked with God. The Almighty was his constant Companion. What would such a walk provide with such a Divine Leader?

You would know His presence and fellowship. His encouragement and counsel. His gentle but clear reproof and perfect correction. You would be trained in righteousness, thoroughly adequate for every good work.

You would be wiser than your enemies, for surely God knows more than anyone or anything and you are beside Him ... hearing His words and gaining His wisdom. You would be taught by the Perfect Teacher.

You would find yourself in the right place at the right time doing the right thing. For those who delight in what God says and stay up with Him are like a "tree planted by rivers of living water that brings forth its fruit in due season; his leaf will not wither and whatever he does will prosper" (Psalm 1).

You would be covered with Almighty protection, for He is your shield and buckler. What could you possibly fear? Who is there to harm you if you are standing beside the Lion of the tribe of Judah? His mighty shoulders towering above you? His arm around you? His eyes staring down your enemies?

Every need would be provided. He would lead you, as your Shepherd, into green pastures and beside still waters. He would restore your soul. He would provide a meal for you in the presence of your enemies. Your cup would run over.

You would be increasingly liberated from sin's intrusion, for if you "walk by the Spirit you will not fulfill the lusts of the flesh," Paul promised.

It is the best life. How could anything be greater, or more advantageous, or sweeter than a lifetime of walking with your Creator and Sustainer, Savior and Friend?

## INTO ETERNITY

It was said of Enoch, Noah's great-grandfather that "Enoch walked with God' and he was not, for God took him" (Genesis 5:24). There comes that day when you are closer to your eternal home than to your earthly residence. And you simply walk with him through "the valley of the shadow of death." He is with you and there is no fear. For you are one of the blessed ones who walks with God.

## DAY 40

# THE BEST PART OF HEAVEN AND EARTH

*Blessed is he who reads and those who hear the words of the prophecy, and heed the things which are written in it; for the time is near.*

*(Revelation 1:3)*

God's Revelation to the Apostle John is our hope. The promises in this book are the foundation for a secure confidence of our future. Although it is hard to understand and interpret in places, we should read it often and deeply. To lose sight of these promises is to lose our perspective, focus, and joy.

## MAKING IT RIGHT

The Revelation unfolds the thunderous roll of God's final judgments. It reminds us that things do get right soon. Those who are sinful and reject God's gracious offer and Christ's incredible sacrifice will pay for this rebellion. Every inequity of this world will be decisively and eternally resolved.

Those who trust Him will be carried into a glory they have not earned and do not deserve, forever to worship in wonder at God's stunning grace. Our lives will be as we've always dreamed and more than our wildest imaginations. Forever without end!

## THE BEST PART

But the most glorious portion of our future will be nothing less than God Himself.

> *Behold, the tabernacle of God is among men, and He will dwell among them, and they shall be His people, and God Himself will be among them. (Revelation 21:3)*

It is this continual, manifest Presence that creates it all. Eternal light, eternal joy, eternal righteousness all flood from the "throne with One seated on it." We will discover that what we have been missing in every area of darkness was God. The ache in our hearts we've continually felt, the longing for more in life, was a longing for Him—not His gifts.

It will become clear to us that everything on earth that was wrong was the absence of His presence. And, that every right moment in our earthly life was brought about by His presence.

The greatest seasons on earth—those glorious times of sweeping revival and awakening—were all created when He would rend the heavens and come down to remind us of what's wrong with this earth and what heaven's rightness is all about. It is Him. He is the satisfaction of our soul's heartache.

## SEEKING HIM NOW

God arms us with this revelation not only to give us hope, but also direction. Our life's work must center on one thing: drawing near to Him and bringing others to Him. We must cooperate with the Spirit to bring people to God—not merely to a building, a program, or a religious system—but to Him.

A believer who is awakened by this vision will repent from self-centeredness and self-seeking. He will be a lifelong repenter as he sees every bit of foolishness that wastes time on himself while ignoring God.

When he realizes that God's presence is the key, he will live the remainder of His days with a passion to experience whatever he can of Him. He will clear the path in any conversation, any environment, so the King of Glory can come in. He will be the sane sage among foolish others who realizes the great need among decaying societies is always God's manifest presence, and He will live and work for that alone.

The more his eyes are filled with this revelation, the more joy will flood his daily life. For he will know that God has made Himself wonderfully accessible now, even though we see through a dark glass. And when a song is sung, or a message preached, or a Scripture read about heaven, he will find himself weeping with delight at the glorious prospect of our near future when God will be among us with no interruption.

## OTHER WRITINGS BY BILL ELLIFF

**The Line of Faith**
*40 Days to Deeper Dependency*
*(Graceful Truth Series, Volume 1)*

**OneCry!**
*A Nationwide Call for Spiritual Awakening*
*With Byron Paulus*

**The Presence Centered Church**

**Whitewater**
*Navigating the Rapids of Church Conflict*

**Forgiveness**
*Healing the Harbored Hurts of your Heart*

**Lifting the Load**
*How to Gain and Maintain a Clear Conscience*

**Everyman** … *the Rescue*

**50 Marks of a Man of God**
*Important questions for those in spiritual leadership*

**Personal Revival Checklist**
*A Spiritual Evaluation through the Sermon on the Mount*

**Turning the Tide**

*Having MORE Kids Who Follow Christ*

(Holly Elliff with Bill Elliff)

To order more copies of *The Essential Presence* or any of our other resources visit www.BillElliff.org

Bulk prices available upon request.